FRESH & TASTY

Casseroles

BARNES
&NOBLE
BOOKS
NEW YORK

Copyright © 2002 by Richard Carroll

This edition published by Barnes & Noble, Inc.,
by arrangement with R&R Publications Marketing Pty. Ltd.

Publisher: Richard Carroll
Creative Director: Paul Sims
Production Manager: Anthony Carroll
Computer Graphics: Lucy Adams
Food Photography: Robert Monro, Warren Webb, Andrew Warn, William Meppem, Andrew Elton,
Quentin Bacon, Gary Smith, Per Ericson
Food Stylists: Ann Fayle, Susan Bell, Coty Hahn, Janet Lodge, Di Kirby
Recipe Development: Ellen Argyriou, Di Kirby, Janet Lodge
Proof Reader: Cindy Brown

Includes index
ISBN 0 7607 3350 3
EAN 9 780760 733509

First edition printed March 2002
Computer Typeset in Garamond, Times New Roman & Humanist

Printed in Singapore

Contents

Introduction

Casseroles meals are popular for three main reasons: they can be prepared ahead of time; they cook without constant attention; and they are quick, tasty, and easy to serve.

Casseroles are based on a blending of the flavors of the ingredients, and most casseroles improve by being prepared in advance. Many can be fixed long before needed and frozen until used. Others lend themselves to being cooked a day in advance and refrigerated until reheated to serve. Casseroles are also excellent for last-minute meals: many can be prepared from ingredients generally found in the cupboard, and can be extended to feed almost any number.

The slow cooking required for many casseroles means that they are an excellent way to utilize less expensive (and less tender) cuts of meat, which will become as tender and tasty as the most expensive steak when cooked slowly for a long time. Casseroles are an ideal way of using leftovers; combined with other ingredients they can present a "new" meal.

Many casseroles contain all the necessary ingredients for a balanced meal—meat, vegetables and sauce—and can be served with a simple salad or crusty bread, thus relieving the cook of last-minute attention to other chores, such as cooking vegetables or preparing a salad.

Casseroles should be served in the containers in which they were cooked; with the large number of attractive ovenproof dishes now available, it should be easy to find one with the right color, shape, and size for your personal preferences. The best part of a casserole, of course, is that it cooks itself. Once all the ingredients are combined (which may be well in advance of cooking), all you have to do is relax and let it cook in the oven or on the stove while you enjoy your guests or family.

Lamb Casseroles

With its tender texture and pleasant taste, no wonder lamb is in a class of its own. Combine lamb with any number of vegetables and spices and you have countless ways to tempt your tastebuds. Whether slow-cooked with macadamias or baked with apricots, you will discover just how versatile this meat can be in your everyday cooking. It is suitable for informal family meals or styling dinner parties as part of a magnificent main. These recipes are sure to be revisited time and time again as you experience each wonderful offering. So fire up your oven because you're in for a treat!

Lamb Shanks with Root Vegetables

Serves 4
Preparation 20 mins
Cooking 1 hr 35 mins
Calories 646
Fat 6½g

2 tbsp olive oil
2 parsnips, peeled, and cut into large chunks
1 medium sweet potato, peeled, and cut into large chunks
1 swede, peeled, and cut into large chunks
1 bunch spring onions, trimmed
2 tbsp olive oil, extra
2 cloves garlic, crushed
4 lamb shanks
³/₄ cup beef stock
¹/₄ cup water
¹/₂ cup red wine
1 tbsp tomato paste
2 sprigs rosemary, chopped
bouquet garni
freshly ground pepper & salt

1 Heat 1 tablespoon oil in a large heavy-based saucepan, add root vegetables, and cook quickly, until brown. Set aside on a plate. Add the extra oil to the pan, and brown the garlic and shanks for a few minutes.
2 To the pan, add the stock, water, red wine, tomato paste, rosemary, bouquet garni, and pepper and salt. Bring to a boil, reduce the heat, and leave to simmer, with the lid on for 20 minutes.
3 Return the vegetables to the pan, and continue to cook for another 30 minutes, until vegetables and lamb are cooked.
4 Before serving, remove the bouquet garni and check the seasoning.

Photograph appears also on page 6

Lamb Hotpot Cooked in Cider

2 tbsp olive oil
4 loin lamb chops
6 lamb's kidneys, halved with
skins and cores removed
1 onion, sliced
1 lb potatoes, sliced
2 carrots, sliced
1 large leek, sliced
2 sticks celery, sliced
salt and black pepper
3 sprigs fresh marjoram or
oregano
1¹/₄ cups dry cider

1 Preheat the oven. Heat one tablespoon of the oil in a large heavy-based frying pan. Add the chops and cook for 1-2 minutes each side, until browned. Remove from the pan, then add the kidneys and cook for 30 seconds on each side or until lightly browned.
2 Arrange half the onion and potatoes in the base of a casserole dish. Top with the chops; add half the carrots, leek and celery, then the kidneys. Add the rest of the carrots, leek and celery, seasoning each layer well. Finish with a layer of onions and potatoes, then tuck in the marjoram or oregano sprigs. Pour over the cider and brush the top with the remaining oil.
3 Cover and cook for 1¹/₂-2 hours, until the meat is tender. Remove the lid, place near the top of the oven and cook for 20-30 minutes, until brown.

OVEN TEMPERATURE
350°F, 180°C, GAS 4

Serves 4
Preparation 25 mins
Cooking 2 hrs 35 mins
Calories 588
Fat 30g

Lamb and Sweet Potato Stew

OVEN TEMPERATURE
450°F, 230°C, GAS 8

Note: A hearty alternative to the traditional hotpot. The fresh herbs make tender lamb cutlets and vegetables extra tasty, but the dish also works with dried herbs.

1 tbsp olive oil
12 lamb cutlets
4 cups lamb or chicken stock
2 onions, thinly sliced
1½ lb sweet potatoes, cut into
½ in thick slices
1¼ cups carrots, chopped
5 sticks celery, chopped
6-7 fresh sage leaves or
1 tsp dried sage
4-5 fresh thyme sprigs or
1 tsp dried thyme
salt and black pepper
3 tbsp pearl barley

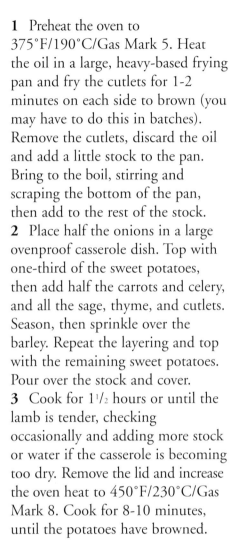

1 Preheat the oven to 375°F/190°C/Gas Mark 5. Heat the oil in a large, heavy-based frying pan and fry the cutlets for 1-2 minutes on each side to brown (you may have to do this in batches). Remove the cutlets, discard the oil and add a little stock to the pan. Bring to the boil, stirring and scraping the bottom of the pan, then add to the rest of the stock.
2 Place half the onions in a large ovenproof casserole dish. Top with one-third of the sweet potatoes, then add half the carrots and celery, and all the sage, thyme, and cutlets. Season, then sprinkle over the barley. Repeat the layering and top with the remaining sweet potatoes. Pour over the stock and cover.
3 Cook for 1½ hours or until the lamb is tender, checking occasionally and adding more stock or water if the casserole is becoming too dry. Remove the lid and increase the oven heat to 450°F/230°C/Gas Mark 8. Cook for 8-10 minutes, until the potatoes have browned.

Serves 6
Preparation 25 mins
Cooking 1 hr 50 mins
Calories 662
Fat 42g

Lamb and Apricot Casserole

1 Preheat the oven. Heat the oil in a flameproof and ovenproof casserole dish on the hob. Add the lamb and cook for about 5 minutes or until browned. Remove and keep warm.

2 Add the onion and garlic to the juices in the dish and cook for 5 minutes or until softened. Return the lamb to the dish with the flour, cilantro, and cumin and cook for 1 minute, stirring. Slowly add the stock and wine and bring to the boil, stirring. Stir in the mushrooms, tomato paste, bouquet garni, and black pepper. Cover and cook in the oven for 1 hour.

3 Stir in the apricots and cook for a further 30 minutes or until the lamb is tender. Remove and discard the bouquet garni, stir in the chopped cilantro, then garnish with more fresh cilantro.

Serves 4
Preparation 15 mins
Cooking 1 hr 45 mins
Calories 374
Fat 14g

1 tbsp sunflower oil
1 lb lean boneless lamb leg or fillet, cut into 1 inch cubes
1 large onion, chopped
1 clove garlic, finely chopped
2 tbsp plain flour
1 tsp ground cilantro
1 tsp ground cumin
1½ cups vegetable stock
½ cup red wine
1 cup baby button mushrooms
1 tbsp tomato paste
1 bouquet garni
black pepper
1½ cups ready-to-eat dried apricots
2 tbsp chopped fresh cilantro, plus extra leaves to garnish

Oven temperature
325°F, 160°C, Gas 3

Note: Dried apricots give a sweetness to this delicious casserole, but dried pears or peaches also work well. Serve it with some steamed broccoli and bread, rice, or jacket potatoes.

Slow Simmered Lamb Shanks with Couscous

OVEN TEMPERATURE
325°F, 160°C, GAS 3

Serves 4
Preparation 20 mins
Cooking 20 mins
Calories 430
Fat 5g

4 Frenched lamb shanks
(ask your butcher to do this)
2 cups canned chopped tomatoes
1 cup red wine
1 bay leaf
6 sprigs fresh thyme
1 cinnamon stick
1½ cups pumpkin, cut into large pieces
2 zucchini, cut into large pieces
8 dried apricots
8 dried prunes
1 cup couscous
2 tbsp flaked almonds, toasted

1 Preheat the oven. Heat a large fry pan over a high heat and sear the lamb shanks in batches until browned all over. Transfer to an ovenproof casserole dish.
2 Add the tomatoes, red wine, bay leaf, thyme, and cinnamon stick. Cover and bake for 1 hour. Add the pumpkin, zucchini, apricots, and prunes, uncover and cook for 30 minutes longer or until the vegetables are soft and the lamb begins to come away from the bone.
3 Put the couscous in a large bowl, pour over 2 cups boiling water and allow to stand for 10 minutes or until all the liquid is absorbed.
4 Serve the lambs shanks in deep bowls on top of the couscous and garnished with flaked almonds.

Slow-Cooked Lamb and Macadamias

1¹/₂ lb boneless leg lamb,
trimmed of visible fat,
cut into 1 inch cubes
¹/₃ cup raisins
¹/₂ cup evaporated skim milk

Spicy Yogurt Marinade
1 white onion, diced
¹/₃ cup ground unsalted
macadamias
1 inch piece fresh ginger, chopped
¹/₂ cup low-fat natural yogurt
2 tsp lime or lemon juice
3 tsp ground cilantro
2 tsp ground cardamom
¹/₂ tsp freshly ground
black pepper

1 Marinade: Place onion, macadamias, ginger, yogurt, and lime juice in a food processor. Process to combine. Stir in cilantro, cardamom and black pepper.
2 Place lamb in a non-reactive dish. Pour over marinade. Toss to coat. Cover. Marinate in the refrigerator overnight.
3 Transfer meat mixture to a heavy-based saucepan. Stir in raisins and evaporated milk. Place pan over a medium heat. Bring to simmering. Reduce heat to low. Cover. Cook, stirring occasionally for 1¹/₂ hours.
4 Remove cover. Cook, stirring occasionally, for 30-40 minutes longer or until meat is tender and sauce is thick. Add a little water during cooking, if necessary.
5 Serve with cooked rice and steamed vegetables of your choice.

Serves 4
Preparation 15 mins
Cooking 2 hrs 15 mins
plus marinating time
Calories 360
Fat 4½g

Lamb Casserole with Couscous and Gremolata

OVEN TEMPERATURE
350°F, 180°C, GAS 4

Note: Gremolata is a mixture of finely chopped herbs, garlic, and citrus rind. Adding this to the casserole, just before serving, lends a fresh new dimension of flavor.

**sea salt and freshly ground
black pepper
2 tbsp plain white flour
4 cups diced lamb, trimmed of
any excess fat
2-3 tbsp extra virgin olive oil
1 yellow and 1 green bell pepper,
deseeded and chopped
2 cups canned chopped tomatoes**

Gremolata
**1 garlic clove, very finely chopped
3 tbsp finely chopped
fresh parsley
grated rind of 1 lemon**

Couscous
**2 cups couscous
1 tbsp extra virgin olive oil
1 large onion, finely sliced**

1 Preheat the oven. Season the flour and place on a large plate, toss the meat until coated. Heat the oil in a large frying pan and cook the meat, over a medium heat, for 2-3 minutes each side, until browned (you will need to do this in two batches). Transfer the browned meat to a casserole dish, using a slotted spoon.

2 Add the peppers to the frying pan and cook for two minutes. Add the tomatoes and bring to a boil. Add these to the lamb and cook in the oven for 40 minutes or until the meat is tender. Meanwhile, mix all the ingredients for the gremolata together.

3 Prepare the couscous according to packet instructions, then fluff up with a fork. Heat the oil in a small frying pan and cook the onion over a medium heat for 10 minutes until golden brown. Add to the couscous and mix well. Sprinkle the gremolata over the lamb casserole and serve with the couscous.

Serves 4
Preparation 30 mins
Cooking 1 hr
Calories 681
Fat 25g

Lamb Osso Bucco

OVEN TEMPERATURE
325°F, 160°C, GAS 3

Note: The lamb is cooked very slowly in this Italian recipe, leaving it meltingly tender, and there should be enough to satisfy the biggest of appetites. Serve with pasta ribbons.

Serves 4
Preparation 15 mins
Cooking 2 hrs 15 mins
Calories 385
Fat 18g

2 tbsp plain flour
salt and black pepper
4 lamb leg shanks, trimmed of excess fat
2 tbsp olive oil
1 onion, finely chopped
1 carrot, finely chopped
1 stick celery, finely chopped
2 cups canned chopped tomatoes with garlic and herbs
1 tbsp sun-dried tomato purée
$^1/_2$ cup dry white wine
2 cups lamb stock

Garnish
1 tbsp chopped fresh parsley
1 tbsp chopped fresh mint
finely grated rind of 1 lemon
1 clove garlic, finely chopped

1 Preheat the oven. Mix together the flour, salt and pepper on a plate. Dip the lamb pieces into the mixture to coat well. Heat 1 tablespoon of the oil in a large heavy-based frying pan until hot but not smoking. Add the coated lamb and cook over a medium to high heat for 5-8 minutes, turning frequently, until browned on all sides. Transfer to a deep ovenproof dish.

2 Heat the remaining oil in the pan, add the onion, carrot, and celery and cook over a low heat for 4-5 minutes, until softened. Add the tomatoes, tomato purée, wine and stock and bring to the boil, stirring occasionally. Pour over the lamb, cover with foil and bake for 1³/₄-2 hours, until the meat is tender, turning it over halfway through. Season to taste.

3 To make the garnish, mix together the parsley, mint, lemon rind and garlic. Sprinkle the garnish over the lamb and serve.

Lamb Shanks with Broad Beans, Olives, and Risoni

Note: If broad beans are large, peel off outer skin.

Serves 4-6
Preparation 8 mins
Cooking 1 hr 15 mins
Calories 678
Fat 4g

2 tbsp olive oil
2 cloves garlic, crushed
4 lamb shanks
1 onion, chopped
2 cups beef stock
4 sprigs oregano
2 tbsp tomato paste
2 cups water
1 cup risoni (rice)
1 cup broad beans
$^1/_2$ cup olives
2 tsp fresh oregano, chopped
salt and freshly ground pepper

1 Heat oil in a large saucepan, add garlic, lamb shanks, and onion, and cook for five minutes (or until shanks are lightly browned).
2 Add the beef stock, sprigs of oregano, tomato paste and half the water, bring to the boil, reduce heat, and leave to simmer (with lid on) for 40 minutes.
3 Remove shanks, slice meat off bone, and set aside.
4 Add the risoni and water, cook for a further five minutes, then add broad beans, olives, meat, oregano, and salt and pepper, cook for five minutes more, and serve.

Sweet Lamb Chop Curry

6 forequarter lamb chops
1 tbsp oil
1 large onion, finely chopped
1 clove garlic, crushed
1½ tbsp Madras-style curry powder
½ tsp ground ginger
2 cups water
salt and pepper
¾ cup mixed dried fruit
1 tsp brown sugar
½ cinnamon stick
½ cup plain yogurt (optional)

1 Trim excess fat from the chops. Wipe over with kitchen paper. Heat oil in a large, heavy-based saucepan or lidded skillet. Add onion and garlic and fry until golden over moderate heat. Remove onion with a slotted spoon, set aside.
2 Increase heat, and brown chops quickly on both sides. Do only 2 or 3 at a time. Remove to plate and drain almost all fat from the pan. Add the curry powder and ginger to the hot saucepan and stir over heat to roast until aroma rises. Stir in the water, lifting the pan juices as you stir. Season with salt and pepper.

3 Return lamb and onion, cover and simmer for 1 hour. Add dried fruit, brown sugar, and cinnamon stick and simmer for approximately 1 hour, until lamb is very soft and tender. Add more water during cooking if necessary.
4 Remove chops to a hot serving platter. Stir yogurt into the sauce (if desired) and pour sauce over the chops. Serve with boiled rice.

Serves 4-6
Preparation 10 mins
Cooking 2 hrs 35 mins
Calories 384
Fat 4g

Bobotie

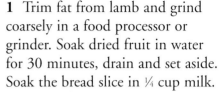

OVEN TEMPERATURE
325°F, 160°C, GAS 3

*A terrific South
African dish which
mixes the taste of
India with the wilds
of South Africa*

Serves 6-8
Preparation 10 mins
plus soaking time
Cooking 1 hr
Calories 361
Fat 6g

2 lb boned leg or
shoulder of lamb
4 large dried peaches, chopped
$^1/_2$ cup seeded raisins, chopped
1 slice white bread
$^1/_4$ cup milk
2 tbsp butter or oil
3 large onions, finely chopped
2 tbsp Madras-style curry
powder
1 tbsp brown sugar
salt and freshly ground black
pepper
$^1/_4$ cup lemon juice
3 eggs
$^1/_4$ cup almonds
4 lemon leaves or bay leaves
$^3/_4$ cup milk, extra

1 Trim fat from lamb and grind coarsely in a food processor or grinder. Soak dried fruit in water for 30 minutes, drain and set aside. Soak the bread slice in ¼ cup milk.
2 Heat butter or oil in a large frying pan, add ground lamb and brown thoroughly, stirring and breaking up lumps with back of a wooden spoon. Remove from pan to a large bowl.
3 Add onions and extra oil to the pan, if needed, and fry onions until soft but not colored. Add curry powder, sugar, salt and pepper, and stir for 1 minute. Stir in lemon juice, dissolving brown pan juices. Bring to the simmer, then pour contents of pan over the meat. Add milk-soaked bread, 1 of the eggs, peaches, raisins, and almonds. Knead with hand to combine all ingredients well.
4 Pack the lamb into a greased baking dish or heatproof lasagna dish and smooth the top. Tuck the lemon or bay leaves beneath the surface of the meat.
5 Beat the 2 remaining eggs with the extra ¾ cup milk, season lightly with salt and pepper, and pour over the surface of the mince. Bake in a preheated slow oven for 40 minutes, until surface is browned and firm. Serve hot with boiled rice.

Lamb and Spinach Curry

2 tbsp vegetable oil
2 onions, chopped
2 cloves garlic, chopped
1 inch piece fresh root ginger,
finely chopped
1 cinnamon stick
1/4 tsp ground cloves
3 cardamom pods
4 cups diced lamb
1 tbsp ground cumin
1 tbsp ground cilantro
4 tbsp natural yogurt
2 tbsp tomato purée
1 cup beef stock
salt and black pepper
3 cups fresh spinach,
finely chopped
2 tbsp roasted flaked almonds

1 Heat the oil in a flameproof casserole dish or a large, heavy-based saucepan. Fry the onions, garlic, ginger, cinnamon, cloves, and cardamom for 5 minutes to soften the onions and garlic, and to release the flavors of the spices.

2 Add the lamb and fry for 5 minutes, turning, until it begins to color. Mix in the cumin and cilantro, then add the yogurt, 1 tablespoon at a time, stirring well each time.

3 Mix together the tomato purée and the stock and add to the lamb. Season to taste. Bring to a boil, then reduce the heat, cover and simmer for 30 minutes or until the lamb is tender.

4 Stir in the spinach, cover and simmer for another 15 minutes, or until the mixture has reduced. Remove the cinnamon stick and the cardamom pods and mix in the almonds.

Note: There's plenty of flavor but no chili in this dish, so it will be a hit even with those who don't like hot curries. You can serve it with pilau or plain rice.

Serves 4
Preparation 15 mins
Cooking 1 hr
Calories 425
Fat 20g

Lamb Korma

Serves 4-6
Preparation 10 mins
Cooking 1 hr 40 mins
Calories 615
Fat 8½g

3 lb shoulder of lamb
salt and freshly
ground black pepper
2 tbsp ghee
1 Spanish onion, finely chopped
1 clove garlic, finely chopped
1 tbsp curry paste
¼ tsp ground ginger
¼ tsp turmeric
⅛ tsp cayenne pepper
2 tbsp flour
1¼ cups chicken stock
¾ cup golden raisins
½ cup yogurt
1 tbsp lemon juice

1 Cut the lamb from the bone into 1½ inch cubes. Season with salt and pepper.
2 Heat ghee in a large, heavy-based saucepan, add ⅓ of the lamb and brown well on all sides. Remove and brown the remainder in 2 batches.
3 Add the onion and garlic and sauté until transparent. Stir in the curry paste, spices, and flour and cook 1 minute. Add the chicken stock, golden raisins and lamb. Cover with a lid and simmer gently for 1 hour or until the lamb is very tender. Stir occasionally during cooking.
4 Stir in the yogurt and lemon juice. Serve with boiled rice and sambals.

Lamb and Apricot Stew

1 Cut peeled tomatoes in half crosswise (through "equator"), gently squeeze out seeds and chop the tomato.
2 Heat half the oil in a heavy-based, lidded frying pan or saucepan, add tomato, peppers, onion and mint, and sauté 5 minutes. Remove from pan.
3 Heat remaining oil, add lamb pieces, stir quickly to brown on all sides. Return vegetables to the pan, add the apricots and enough water to almost cover the meat. Bring to a boil, turn down heat, and simmer 1 hour.
4 After the hour season with salt and pepper. Check liquid content and add more if needed. Simmer one hour more, until lamb is very tender. Serve with boiled rice.

**4 ripe tomatoes,
blanched and peeled
2 tbsp oil
1 green bell pepper, seeded and
finely chopped
1 large onion, chopped
2 tbsp fresh mint, chopped
6 cups lamb cubes, cut from
the leg or shoulder
²/₃ cup dried apricots
salt and freshly
ground black pepper**

Serves 6
Preparation 8 mins
Cooking 1 hr 20 mins
Calories 335
Fat 3⅓g

Lancashire Hotpot

OVEN TEMPERATURE
400°F, 200°C, GAS 6

Note: Layers of potato, onions, and carrots sandwich tender loin chops in this traditional hotpot. It's a meal in itself —all it needs is a glass of ale or cider to wash it down.

Serves 4
Preparation 20 mins
Cooking 1 hr 20 mins
Calories 617
Fat 35g

3 tbsp butter or dripping
4 large lamb loin chops or
8 lamb cutlets, trimmed
1¹/₂ lb potatoes, thinly sliced
2 large onions, sliced
3 large carrots, sliced
salt and black pepper
2 cups lamb stock

1 Preheat the oven. Heat 2 tablespoons of the butter or dripping in a frying pan and cook the chops or cutlets for 5 minutes on each side to brown. Arrange half the potatoes in a large casserole dish, and top with half the onions, then half the carrots, seasoning each layer lightly. Add the chops or cutlets and a final layer each of onions, carrots, and potatoes, again seasoning each layer. Pour over the stock, then dot with the remaining butter or dripping.

2 Cover the casserole and cook for 30 minutes. Reduce the oven temperature to 300°F/150°C/ Gas Mark 2 and cook for a further hour. Increase the oven temperature to 400°F/200°C/Gas Mark 6, then uncover the dish and cook for 30-40 minutes, until the potatoes have browned.

Georgian Lamb Stew

Serves 4
Preparation 10 mins
Cooking 1 hr 15 mins
Calories 474
Fat 2¼g

1½ lb lamb chump chops
1 large onion, chopped
2 cups canned peeled tomatoes,
drained
2 lb potatoes, peeled and cut into
¾ in pieces
salt and freshly ground pepper
½ cup coarsely chopped fresh
cilantro leaves, mint leaves, basil
leaves, dill sprigs and parsley
leaves
½ tsp cayenne pepper
4 cloves garlic

1 Remove bones and cut lamb into large pieces, leaving any visible fat on the meat.
2 In a large saucepan, cook lamb over low heat, stirring frequently for 10 minutes, or until it is no longer pink. Add onion and cook mixture over moderately low heat, stirring occasionally, until the onion is softened. Add tomatoes (breaking them up with a wooden spoon), potatoes, and a pinch of salt and freshly ground pepper, and simmer the mixture, half-covered, stirring occasionally for 40 minutes or until lamb and potatoes are tender.
3 Add the herb mixture and cayenne, stirring, and simmer the stew for a further 4 minutes. Stir in the garlic and remove the stew from the heat. Let the stew stand, covered, for 5 minutes and season with salt and pepper before serving.

Lamb and Barley Casserole

4 tbsp butter
1 onion, sliced
2 sticks celery, sliced
$^1/_2$ cup mushrooms, sliced,
optional
1$^1/_2$ lb neck chops
1$^1/_2$ cups pearl barley,
washed and drained
2 cups hot stock
2 cups canned peeled tomatoes
salt and freshly
ground black pepper
chopped parsley
2 tbsp grated
Parmesan cheese

1 Melt butter in a heavy flameproof casserole. Saute onion, celery, and optional mushrooms for about 5 minutes. Add chops and saute, until they change color. Add barley, stir and add hot stock and tomatoes, including juice. Cover and bake in a moderately slow oven for 1-1$^1/_2$ hours.

2 Check once or twice during cooking time and add more stock or water if barley is dry. Season to taste with salt and pepper. Before serving, sprinkle with chopped parsley and cheese.

OVEN TEMPERATURE
350°F, 180°C, GAS 4

Serves 6
Preparation 6 mins
Cooking 1 hr 50 mins
Calories 462
Fat 7g

Beef Casseroles

Beef has been baked, braised, curried, stewed, and fried and still new recipes are uncovered to make the world's carnivores rediscover one of the world's long-standing staples. We have compiled a fresh range of recipes for your eating enjoyment. Stir up beef with shallots in our tasty stew, bake beef in pies with a splash of Guinness, or simmer beef to make a classic Indonesian curry–you will be surprised how many facets there are to this wonderful meat. No longer will you be stuck serving steak-and-veggies at your meal table, because beef has never seen so many applications.

Slowly Simmered Indonesian Beef Curry

Photograph also appears on page 27

Note: Rendang, a classic Indonesian dish, can also be made with lamb or venison. Slow cooking in the rich coconut sauce results in meltingly tender meat. Serve with rice.

Serves 4
Preparation 25 mins
Cooking 3 hrs 15 mins
Calories 462
Fat 38g

2 stalks lemon grass
4 tbsp desiccated coconut
2 onions, chopped
2 cloves garlic, chopped
2 inch piece fresh root ginger, chopped
1 red chili, deseeded and chopped, plus 1 red chili, deseeded and sliced, to garnish
2 tbsp vegetable oil
1½ lb top loin steak, cut into 1in cubes
1 tsp turmeric
1½ cups canned coconut milk
1 tsp sugar
salt

1 Peel the outer layers from the lemon grass stalks, then finely chop the lower white bulbous parts discarding the fibrous tops. Heat a large saucepan and dry-fry the coconut for 5 minutes or until golden, stirring frequently. Finely grind the coconut in a food processor or use a pestle and mortar.

2 Blend or grind the lemon grass, onions, garlic, ginger, and chili to a paste. Heat the oil in the pan and fry the paste for 5 minutes to release the flavors, stirring often. Add the beef, stir to coat and fry for 3-4 minutes, until sealed.

3 Add the ground coconut, turmeric, coconut milk, sugar, and salt to taste and mix well. Bring to the boil, stirring, then reduce the heat. Simmer, uncovered, for 3 hours, stirring from time to time, until the sauce reduces to a rich gravy. Garnish with the sliced chili.

Beef Braised in Rioja

3 tbsp olive oil
1¹/₂ lb stewing beef, trimmed of fat and cut into 2¹/₂ in chunks
6 shallots, finely chopped
2 garlic cloves, crushed
2 sticks celery, thickly sliced
1¹/₂ cups mushrooms, thickly sliced
¹/₂ tsp ground allspice
¹/₂ bottle full-bodied red wine
1 cup tomato paste
2 sprigs fresh thyme
salt and black pepper

1 Preheat the oven. Heat the oil in a flameproof casserole dish or large saucepan and fry the meat over a high heat, stirring, for 5-10 minutes, until browned. Remove from the pan, then add the shallots, garlic, and celery. Cook, stirring, for 3-4 minutes, until lightly browned.
2 Add the mushrooms and cook for 1 minute or until softened. Stir in the allspice, wine, tomato paste, 1 sprig of thyme and season. Return the meat to the dish or pan and bring the mixture to a simmer.
3 Cover and cook in the oven or over a low heat on the hob for 1¹/₂-2 hours, until the beef is tender. Season again if necessary, then serve garnished with the remaining thyme.

OVEN TEMPERATURE
350°F, 180°C, GAS 4

Note: This Spanish casserole is perfect on a cold day, served with garlic mash. You can use any type of mushroom, but ceps or chestnut ones are especially good.

Serves 4
Preparation 20 mins
Cooking 2 hrs 14 mins
Calories 487
Fat 28g

Mexican-Style Beef Olives

OVEN TEMPERATURE
300°F, 150°C, GAS 2

Serves 4
Preparation 20 mins
Cooking 1 hr 45 mins
Calories 433
Fat 19g

4 thin-cut beef steaks
4 rashers rindless bacon, finely chopped
1 tbsp chopped fresh parsley
$\frac{1}{2}$ tsp dried marjoram
1 cup fresh breadcrumbs
3 tbsp plain flour
salt and black pepper
1 tbsp vegetable oil
1-2 tsp hot chili powder
1 onion, chopped
2 cloves garlic, finely chopped
1 red bell pepper, deseeded and chopped
1 cup beef stock
$1\frac{1}{2}$ cups red kidney beans, drained and rinsed

1 Place the beef between sheets of cling film and flatten slightly with a rolling pin. Put the bacon into a large frying pan and fry gently for 2-3 minutes, until cooked. Remove from the heat and stir in the parsley, marjoram, and breadcrumbs.

2 Mix together the flour, salt and pepper in a shallow dish. Divide the bacon mixture between the slices of beef, then roll up each slice from the short end, turn in the seasoned flour and secure with a wetted cocktail stick.

3 Heat the oil in a flameproof casserole dish, add the beef and cook for 2 minutes, turning until browned all over. Remove from the dish and set aside. Add the chili powder, onion, garlic and red pepper to the dish and cook for 3 minutes to soften. Return the meat to the dish, pour in the stock, then bring to the boil. Cover the dish, then bake for 45 minutes. Add the kidney beans and cook for another 45 minutes. Remove the cocktail sticks and serve.

Rich Beef Stew with Shallots

6 shallots, quartered
6 large cloves garlic, quartered
3 large carrots, sliced
4 sticks celery, sliced
4 tbsp olive oil
2¹/₂ lb lean stewing beef, cut into
2 inch cubes
few thyme sprigs, 1 bay leaf,
1 rosemary sprig and 1 strip of
lemon rind, tied with string
2 cups full-bodied red wine
1 cups beef stock
3 tbsp pearl barley
10 black peppercorns, crushed
salt and black pepper

Serves 6
Preparation 20 mins
Cooking 3 hrs 10 mins
Calories 471
Fat 21g

OVEN TEMPERATURE
475°F, 240°C, GAS 9

*Note:
There are times
when all you want
is a warming stew,
especially if the
weather is bad.
Serve with
comforting mashed
potato with chopped
fresh parsley stirred in.*

1 Preheat the oven. Place the shallots, garlic, carrots, and celery in a roasting tin, pour over 2 tablespoons of oil, then mix well. Cook for 15 minutes, turning frequently, or until the vegetables are browned.

2 Heat the remaining oil in a large, heavy-based saucepan, add one-third of the meat and fry for 5-8 minutes, until browned all over. Remove from the pan and set aside while you cook the remaining meat in two more batches. Return all the meat to the dish. Add the vegetables, herb bundle, wine, stock, pearl barley, and peppercorns. Season and bring to the boil.

3 Reduce the heat and simmer, partly covered, for 2-2¹/₂ hours, until the meat is tender. Check from time to time and add a little more stock or water if the stew starts to dry out. Remove the herb bundle before serving.

Beef Carbonade

2-3 tbsp vegetable oil
2 lb braising or stewing steak, cut
into 1 in cubes
1 large onion, thinly sliced
1 tbsp plain flour
2 tbsp soft dark brown sugar
1 can Guinness
2 cups beef stock
1 tbsp tomato purée
1 bouquet garni
salt and black pepper
fresh parsley to garnish

Oven temperature
325°F, 160°C, Gas 3

*Note: Almost
everyone loves a
good old-fashioned
stew, and you can't
beat a beef one.
Serve it with plenty
of creamy mashed
potatoes to soak up
the rich gravy.*

Serves 4
Preparation 15 mins
Cooking 2 hrs 30 mins
Calories 506
Fat 20g

1 Preheat the oven. Heat 2
tablespoons of the oil in a
flameproof casserole dish. Add a
third of the beef and fry over
a high heat for 6-7 minutes, turning
until browned on all sides.
Remove from the pan while you cook
the remaining batches, adding more
oil if necessary. Set the beef aside.
2 Lower the heat, add the onion
and cook for 5 minutes, stirring.
Sprinkle in the flour and sugar and
stir for 1-2 minutes, then pour in
the stout and beef stock and bring
to a boil, stirring. Return the beef
to the dish and add the tomato purée
and bouquet garni. Season and stir well,
then cover.
3 Transfer the dish to the oven and
cook for 1½-2 hours, until the beef
is tender and cooked through. Stir
2-3 times during cooking, adding a
little water if necessary. Discard the
bouquet garni and season again if
necessary. Garnish with parsley.

Steak and Kidney Puffs

Oven temperature
325°F, 160°C, Gas 3

Note: These puffs have all the flavor of a steak and kidney pie, but they're much lighter and very easy to prepare.

Serves 4
Preparation 20 mins
Cooking 2 hrs 50 mins
Calories 650
Fat 35g

4 tbsp groundnut oil
1 onion, finely chopped
1 lb braising steak, trimmed of excess fat and cubed
³/₄ lb pig's kidney, halved, cores removed, then cut into ¹/₂ in pieces
3 tbsp plain flour
1 tbsp tomato purée
2 tsp Worcestershire sauce
1¹/₂ cups beef stock
finely grated rind of 1 lemon
2 tbsp finely chopped fresh parsley, plus extra to garnish
1 tsp dried mixed herbs
salt and black pepper
¹/₂ cup baby button mushrooms
1 pack ready-rolled puff pastry
fresh rosemary to garnish

1 Preheat the oven. Heat half the oil in a large flameproof casserole dish, add the onion and cook for 5 minutes. Add half the steak and kidney and fry over a high heat, stirring, for 6 minutes or until browned. Keep warm. Fry the remaining meat, adding more oil if necessary.

2 Return all the meat to the dish, add the flour and stir for 2 minutes. Add the tomato purée, Worcestershire sauce, stock, lemon rind, herbs, and salt and pepper. Bring to a boil, stirring, then cover.

3 Transfer to the oven. After 1¹/₂ hours, stir in the mushrooms and a little water, if needed. Cook for 35 minutes more. Meanwhile, unroll the pastry and cut into 4 x 4¹/₂ inch circles. Put on a baking sheet.

4 Take the casserole out of the oven. Increase the oven temperature to 400°F/200°C/Gas Mark 6. Meanwhile, place the casserole over a very low heat. Keep covered but stir occasionally. Bake the pastry for 20 minutes or until golden brown. Top each pastry circle with the steak and kidney. Garnish with herbs.

Individual Beef and Red Wine Pies

1 Preheat the oven. You will need 6 2-cup capacity ovenproof pie dishes.

2 Heat the oil in a large pot, add the onion and cook over a medium heat for 5 minutes, or until golden. Add the garlic and the beef and cook for 5 minutes until the beef is browned.

3 Add the flour and tomato paste and cook for a further 2 minutes, stirring constantly. Stir in the red wine and stock, and bring to a boil. Add the carrots, mushrooms and chopped thyme. Reduce the heat, cover, and simmer for about 1 hour, then remove the lid and cook for a further 45 minutes until the beef is tender and the sauce is reduced and thickened. Stir through the parsley, transfer to a bowl, and allow the filling to cool completely.

4 Using the top of a pie dish as a guide, cut 6 circles from the pastry, about $^3/_4$ inches larger than the dish. Spoon the cooled filling into the dishes. Brush the edges of each pastry circle with a little water then cover the dishes (damp side down), pressing the pastry to the side of the dish to seal. Cut a small cross in the top of each pie, insert a sprig of thyme, and lightly brush with milk.

5 Bake for 20-25 minutes or until the pastry is crisp and golden and the filling is hot. Serve the pies with mashed potato and steamed beans.

2 tsp peanut oil
1 large onion, chopped
2 cloves garlic, crushed
2 lb beef steak, trimmed of all fat and cubed
2 tbsp plain flour
2 tbsp reduced salt
2 tbsp tomato paste
1$^1/_2$ cups red wine
1$^1/_2$ cups reduced salt beef stock
2 carrots, thinly sliced
2 cups Swiss brown mushrooms, quartered
2 tbsp fresh thyme, chopped
2 tbsp fresh parsley, chopped
2 sheets puff pastry, defrosted
4 sprigs thyme
1 tbsp low or reduced fat milk

OVEN TEMPERATURE
400°F, 200°C, GAS 6

Serves 6
Preparation 30 mins plus cooling
Cooking 2 hrs 30 mins
Calories 325
Fat 8g

Mediterranean Beef and Olive Casserole

OVEN TEMPERATURE
325°F, 160°C, GAS 3

Note: Long, slow cooking makes this beef steak gloriously tender. Black olives and fresh fennel lend their distinctive flavors to the rich wine and tomato sauce.

Serves 6
Preparation 30 mins plus 4 hrs marinating
Cooking 3hrs 15 mins
Calories 474
Fat 16g

grated rind and juice of 1 lemon
3 lb lean braising steak, cut into 2 inch chunks
2 tbsp olive oil
3 tbsp drained pitted black olives, plus 15 unpitted to serve
4 tomatoes, quartered and deseeded
salt and black pepper
chopped fresh parsley to garnish

Marinade
2 medium onions, chopped
2 cloves garlic, crushed
3 bay leaves
3 fresh thyme sprigs or 2 tsp dried thyme
1 tsp dried oregano
2 tbsp chopped fresh parsley
1 small bulb fennel, chopped
2 carrots, sliced
8 black peppercorns
2 tbsp olive oil
1 bottle dry white wine

1 Fill a large non-metallic bowl with cold water and add the lemon juice. Rinse the meat in the lemon water then drain well. Mix together all the ingredients for the marinade, then add the meat and coat. Cover and refrigerate for 4 hours, or overnight.

2 Preheat the oven. Lift the meat out of the bowl, reserving the marinade, and drain well. Coat a large, flameproof and ovenproof casserole dish with one tablespoon of oil. Add half the meat and fry for 6-7 minutes, until browned, turning once. Set aside, then fry the remaining meat. Stir in the marinade and the pitted olives and mix well.

3 Cover the dish with a double layer of foil, then a lid. Cook for 2 hours. Remove the lid and foil, press the meat down with the back of a wooden spoon and top with the tomatoes. Season lightly and drizzle over the remaining oil. Cover the dish with the foil and lid again and cook for 1 hour or until the beef is tender.

4 Skim off any surface fat. Season if necessary, then sprinkle over the lemon rind, the parsley, and the whole olives. Serve from the dish.

Jarkoy

1 Trim the fat from the chuck steak. Cut into large cubes. Peel and slice the carrots and onions. Heat a large heavy-based saucepan, add butter or oil, and a third of the beef cubes. Toss to brown well on all sides over high heat. Remove and brown the remainder in 2 batches. Add the sliced carrot and onions and sauté a little.

2 Return all meat to saucepan and sprinkle in the flour to cover all the surface. Add the garlic, dill, nutmeg, salt, pepper, and beef stock. Bring to a boil over high heat, stirring to lift browned-on juices. Cover, reduce heat to low and simmer slowly for 1½ hours.

3 After 1½ hours add dried fruits, mint and cilantro. Cover and simmer 30 minutes more, or until meat is tender. Remove to a heated serving dish. Sprinkle with crushed walnuts and orange juice.

2 lb thick-cut beef steak
3 large carrots
3 medium onions, thinly sliced
2 tbsp butter or oil
2 tbsp flour
2 cloves garlic, crushed
1 tsp chopped fresh dill
or $^1/_2$ tsp dried
$^1/_2$ tsp nutmeg, grated or ground
salt and freshly
ground black pepper
1$^1/_2$ cups rich beef stock
$^1/_2$ cup dried apricots
$^1/_2$ cup dried peaches,
cut in quarters
$^1/_2$ cup pitted prunes
1 tsp chopped mint
1 tbsp chopped cilantro
$^1/_2$ cup walnuts, crushed
$^1/_4$ cup orange juice

Serves 6
Preparation 10 mins
Cooking 2 hrs 30 mins
Calories 449
Fat 7g

Steak Pie with Guinness

Note: Guinness adds its creamy richness to this slow-cooked steak pie. Serve it with mash and peas or cabbage.

Serves 6
Preparation 30 mins
Cooking 2 hrs
Calories 628
Fat 32g

1 Preheat the oven. Combine the flour, mustard, and pepper, then coat the beef in the mixture. Heat 2 tablespoons of oil in a heavy- based frying pan. Fry a third of the beef for 3-4 minutes, until browned. Transfer to an ovenproof dish and fry the rest of the beef in 2 more batches.
2 Add another tablespoon of oil to the pan, then fry the onions for 5 minutes. Add the garlic and cook for 2 minutes. Stir in the Guinness, Worcestershire sauce, herbs, and sugar, and simmer for 2-3 minutes. Pour over the beef, then cover and cook in the oven for 2 hours. Remove the beef and increase the oven temperature to 375°F/190°C/ Gas Mark 5. Fry the mushrooms in the rest of the oil. Stir into the beef, then transfer to a 6x8 inch pie dish.
3 Sift together the flour, baking powder and $1/2$ teaspoon of salt, then add the thyme and pepper. Stir in the suet and bind with 10-12 tablespoons of water to form a soft dough. Roll it out, dampen the edges of the dish and cover with the pastry. Trim, then make a small slit in the center. Cook for 30-40 minutes, until golden.

3 tbsp plain flour
1 tsp English mustard powder
salt and black pepper
2 lb stewing beef, trimmed and cut into cubes
4 tbsp vegetable oil
2 onions, sliced
2 cloves garlic, finely chopped
2 cups Guinness
2 tbsp Worcestershire sauce
2 bay leaves
1 tbsp chopped fresh thyme
1 tsp soft dark brown sugar
1 cup chestnut mushrooms, halved if large

Pastry Crust
2 cups plain flour
$1/2$ tsp baking powder
2 tsp chopped fresh thyme
$1/2$ cup shredded suet

Beef and Mushroom Pie

OVEN TEMPERATURE
375°F, 190°C, GAS 5

Note: Homemade puff pastry takes a little time to make, but the result is well worth it.

Serves 4
Preparation 35 mins
Cooking 2 hrs 30 mins
Calories 1294
Fat 37g

Puff Pastry
6 tbsp butter, softened
6 tbsp lard, softened
2 cups plain flour
¹/₂ cup cold water

Beef and Mushroom Filling
2 lb lean beef, cut into
1 inch cubes
¹/₄ cup seasoned flour
6 tbsp butter
3 tbsp olive oil
2 onions, chopped
2 cloves garlic, crushed
2 cups button mushrooms, sliced
¹/₂ cup red wine
¹/₂ cup beef stock
1 bay leaf
2 tbsp finely chopped fresh parsley
1 tbsp Worcestershire sauce
freshly ground black pepper
1 tbsp cornstarch blended with
2 tbsp water
1 egg, lightly beaten

1 To make filling, toss meat in flour to coat. Shake off excess flour. Melt butter and oil in a large heavy-based saucepan and cook meat in batches for 3-4 minutes, or until browned on all sides. Remove meat from pan and set aside.

2 Add onions and garlic to pan and cook over a medium heat for 3-4 minutes, or until onion softens. Stir in mushrooms and cook for 2 minutes longer. Combine wine and stock, pour into pan and cook for 4-5 minutes, stirring constantly to lift sediment from base of pan. Bring to a boil, then reduce heat. Return meat to pan with bay leaf, parsley, Worcestershire sauce, and black pepper to taste. Cover and simmer for 1¹/₂ hours or until meat is tender. Stir in cornstarch mixture and cook, stirring, until mixture thickens. Remove pan from heat and set aside to cool.

3 To make pastry, place butter and lard in a bowl and mix until well combined. Cover and refrigerate until firm. Place flour in a large mixing bowl. Cut one-quarter of butter mixture into small pieces and rub into flour using fingertips until mixture resembles coarse bread crumbs. Mix in enough water to form a firm dough.

4 Turn pastry onto a floured surface and knead lightly. Roll pastry out to a 6x10 in rectangle. Cut another one-quarter of butter mixture into small pieces and place over top two-thirds of pastry. Fold the bottom third of pastry up and top third of pastry down to give three even layers. Half turn pastry to have open end facing you, and roll out to a rectangle as before. Repeat folding and rolling twice. Cover pastry and refrigerate for 1 hour.

5 Place cooled filling in a 4 cup oval pie dish. On a lightly floured surface, roll out pastry 1¹/₂ in larger than pie dish. Cut off a ¹/₂ in strip from pastry edge. Brush rim of dish with water and press pastry strip onto rim. Brush pastry strip with water. Lift pastry top over filling and press gently to seal edges. Trim and knock back edges to make a decorative edge. Brush with egg and bake for 30 minutes or until pastry is golden and crisp.

Daube of Beef

Serves 4
Preparation 8 mins
Cooking 2 hrs 50 mins
Calories 637
Fat 8g

2 lb chuck or blade steak,
trimmed of all visible fat
and cubed
1/2 cup seasoned flour
1/4 cup olive oil
1 onion, chopped
1 clove garlic, crushed
1 leek, sliced
2 cups beef stock
1 cup red wine
1 tsp dried mixed herbs
freshly ground black pepper
1 bay leaf
few thin strips orange rind
(optional)
2 zucchini, sliced
1 large sweet potato, chopped
1 parsnip, sliced

1 Toss beef in flour. Shake off excess and set aside. Heat half the oil in a large frying pan over a medium heat and cook beef in batches for 3-4 minutes or until brown. Place in a casserole dish.

2 Heat remaining oil in same pan, add onion and garlic, and cook over a medium heat, stirring, for 4-5 minutes. Add leek and cook for 2-3 minutes longer. Add vegetables to casserole dish.

3 Add stock, wine, herbs, and black pepper to taste to pan and, stirring, bring to a boil. Reduce heat and simmer until liquid reduces by half. Add stock mixture, bay leaf, and orange rind, if using, to casserole dish and bake for 1 1/2-2 hours, or until beef is tender.

4 Add zucchinis, sweet potato and parsnip and bake for extra 30 minutes or until vegetables are tender.

Venison Casserole with Chili Beans

1 Preheat the oven. Mix together the flour, salt and pepper on a plate. Dip the venison into the mixture to coat. Heat the oil in a large flameproof casserole dish and fry the venison in batches over a medium to high heat for 5 minutes, or until browned on all sides. Remove from the pan and set aside.

2 Lower the heat and add the onion to the dish with a little more oil, if necessary. Stir for 5 minutes or until lightly browned, then add the garlic, chilies, and chili powder and stir for 1 minute.

3 Add the tomatoes, beef stock, tomato purée, and sugar. Bring to a boil, stirring. Add the venison, stir well, and cover tightly with the lid. Transfer the dish to the oven and cook for 2 hours or until the venison is tender, stirring twice and adding the kidney beans for the last 30 minutes of cooking.

2 tbsp plain flour
salt and black pepper
1¹/₂ lb diced shoulder of venison
2 tbsp groundnut oil
1 Spanish onion, finely chopped
2 cloves garlic, crushed
2 fresh green chilies, deseeded and finely chopped
1 tbsp chili powder
2 cups canned chopped tomatoes
2 cups beef stock
2 tbsp tomato purée
2 tsp soft light or dark brown sugar
2 cups canned red kidney beans, drained and rinsed

OVEN TEMPERATURE
300°F, 150°C, GAS 2

Note: Tender chunks of slow-cooked venison are set off by a spicy mixture of beans and tomatoes in this casserole. Serve with rice or crusty bread and a large salad.

Serves 4
Preparation 20 mins
Cooking 2 hrs 50 mins
Calories 427
Fat 10g

Spiced Shredded Beef

Note: Wholewheat
pasta and fresh
vegetables are high
in soluble fiber.
As part of a
balanced diet,
soluble fiber can
help to lower
cholesterol levels.
It binds with
cholesterol and so
makes it easier for
the body to get rid
of it as waste.

Serves 6
Preparation 8 mins
Cooking 2 hrs
Calories 236
Fat 3g

$1^{1}/_{2}$ **lb boneless beef chuck,**
blade or brisket, trimmed of
visible fat
1 onion, halved
2 cloves garlic, peeled
1 clove
2 tsp cumin seeds
8 cups water

Green Chili and Tomato Sauce
2 tsp vegetable oil
1 onion, chopped
2 hot green chilies, chopped
2 cups canned tomatoes,
undrained and chopped

1 Place beef, onion, garlic, clove, cumin seeds and water in a saucepan over a medium heat, bring to simmering and simmer, skimming the top occasionally, for $1^{1}/_{2}$ hours or until beef is very tender. Remove pan from heat and cool beef in liquid. Skim fat from surface as it cools. Remove beef from liquid and shred with a fork. Reserve cooking liquid for making sauce.
2 To make sauce, heat oil in a frying pan over a high heat, add onion and chilies and cook, stirring, for 3 minutes or until tender. Stir in tomatoes and 1 cup of the reserved cooking liquid, bring to simmering and simmer for 10 minutes, or until mixture reduces and thickens.
3 Add shredded beef to sauce and simmer for 5 minutes or until heated through.

Belgian Beef Casserole

1½ lb chuck or blade steak, cubed
2 tbsp dripping or other fat
2 onions, sliced
1 tbsp flour
1 cup beer
1 cup hot beef stock
1 clove garlic, crushed
1 bouquet garni
salt and freshly ground black
pepper
½ tsp nutmeg
½ tsp sugar
1 tsp vinegar
8 slices French bread, ¾ in thick
French mustard

OVEN TEMPERATURE
325°F, 160°C, GAS 3

Serves 4-6
Preparation 5 mins
Cooking 2 hrs 50 mins
Calories 329
Fat 5g

1 Brown meat in hot dripping in flameproof casserole, then lower heat and add onions. Cook for 2 minutes. Sprinkle with flour, pour on beer and hot stock and stir until boiling. Add garlic, bouquet garni, salt, pepper, nutmeg, sugar, and vinegar. Cover and cook in a preheated moderately slow oven for 2 hours or until meat is tender.

2 Remove casserole from oven, remove bouquet garni. Skim off fat and spoon it over bread slices, then spread bread thickly with mustard. Arrange on top of casserole, pushing bread well into gravy (it will float again to the top). Cook uncovered for a further 30 minutes or until bread forms a good brown crust.

White Meat Casseroles

Chicken, turkey, pork, rabbit, veal—white meat comes in all shapes and sizes, providing a wonderful array of possibilities when it lands on your kitchen counter. Braised pork, for example, is a perfect match to the tartness of apples, while chicken curry is a marvelous companion to Jasmine rice. The introduction of multiple spices and seasonings into the equation means this journey becomes even more interesting. You will lose yourself in these pages as they inspire you to reignite your originality at the next family meal or special function. It's all at your fingertips…

Spanish Chicken with Chorizo

Note: Packed with Mediterranean flavors, this casserole is equally good eaten with rice or crusty bread. You can use stock or orange juice instead of the sherry or vermouth.

Serves 4
Preparation 15 mins
Cooking 55 mins
Calories 443
Fat 31g

8 chicken joints, such as thighs and drumsticks
2 tbsp olive oil
1 onion, sliced
2 cloves garlic, crushed
1 red and 1 yellow bell pepper, deseeded and sliced
2 tsp paprika
3 tbsp cup dry sherry or dry vermouth
2 cups canned chopped tomatoes
1 bay leaf
1 strip orange rind, pared with a vegetable peeler
1 cup chorizo, sliced
1/3 cup pitted black olives
salt and black pepper

1 Place the chicken joints in a large non-stick frying pan and fry without oil for 5-8 minutes, turning occasionally, until golden. Remove the chicken and set aside, then pour away any fat from the pan.
2 Add the oil to the pan and fry the onion, garlic and peppers for 3-4 minutes, until softened. Return the chicken to the pan with the paprika, sherry or vermouth, tomatoes, bay leaf, and orange rind. Bring to a boil, then simmer, covered, over a low heat for 35-40 minutes, stirring occasionally, until the chicken is cooked through.
3 Add the chorizo and olives and simmer for a further 5 minutes to heat through, then season.

Photograph appears also on page 46

Turkey and Mushroom Creole

1 tbsp olive oil
1 onion, chopped
2 cloves garlic, chopped
1 red bell pepper, deseeded and chopped
2 sticks celery, chopped
2 cups canned chopped tomatoes
1 tsp chili powder
large pinch of cayenne pepper
1 tsp paprika
$^1/_2$ tsp dried thyme
1 lb quick-cook turkey steaks, cut into strips
1 cup button mushrooms, sliced

1   Heat the oil in a large heavy-based saucepan, then add the onion, garlic, red pepper, and celery and cook gently for 10 minutes or until softened.
2   Stir in the tomatoes, chili, cayenne, paprika, and thyme and heat through for 1-2 minutes to release the flavors. Stir in the turkey strips and mushrooms, then cover the pan and cook gently for 30 minutes, stirring occasionally, until the turkey is cooked through and tender.

Note: This West Indian-inspired dish tastes great and it's really healthy too. Serve it with some rice to soak up the spicy tomato and mushroom sauce.

Serves 4
Preparation 20 mins
Cooking 45 mins
Calories 198
Fat 5g

Braised Pork with Apples

OVEN TEMPERATURE
420°F, 210°C, GAS 7

Note: Pork goes beautifully with the slight tartness of cooked apples. In this succulent slow-cooked casserole, the cider brings out the taste of the apples even more.

Serves 4
Preparation 15 mins
Cooking 45 mins
Calories 242
Fat 11g

1 tbsp sunflower oil
4 boneless lean pork loin
steaks or loin medallions
4 shallots, thinly sliced
1 cup mushrooms, sliced
1 tbsp plain flour
1 cup vegetable stock
$^1/_2$ cup dry cider
2 tsp Dijon or
wholegrain mustard
black pepper
2 large eating apples,
peeled, cored and sliced
fresh flat-leaf parsley to garnish

1 Preheat the oven. Heat the oil in a non-stick frying pan. Add the pork and cook for 5 minutes or until browned, turning once, then transfer to a casserole dish.
2 Add the shallots and mushrooms to the frying pan and cook gently for 5 minutes or until softened. Add the flour and cook for 1 minute, stirring. Slowly add the stock and cider, stirring until smooth, then add the mustard and black pepper. Bring to the boil and continue stirring for 2-3 minutes, until thickened.
3 Place the apple slices on top of the pork steaks and pour over the sauce. Cover and cook in the oven for 1-1$^1/_4$ hours, until the pork is tender and cooked through. Garnish with fresh parsley.

Light Chicken Curry with Jasmine Rice

2 cups reduced fat coconut milk
1 cup reduced salt chicken stock
2-3 tbsp green curry paste
3 kaffir lime leaves, finely shredded
1¹/₂ cups pumpkin, peeled and chopped
4 skinless chicken breast fillets, cut into small cubes
small can bamboo shoots, drained
1 cup snake beans, chopped
1 cup broccoli, cut into florets
1 tbsp fish sauce
1 tbsp palm sugar, grated
2 tbsp Thai basil leaves, torn

Jasmine Rice
1¹/₂ cups jasmine rice
2 stalks lemon grass, halved

1 Put the coconut milk, stock, green curry paste and kaffir lime leaves in wok or large pot and bring to a boil. Cook over a high heat until the sauce starts to thicken slightly. Add the pumpkin and simmer for 10 minutes, or until it starts to soften.

2 Add the chicken breast and bamboo shoots, reduce the heat and simmer for 10 minutes, or until the chicken is tender. Add the snake beans, broccoli, fish sauce, and palm sugar, and cook uncovered until the vegetables are soft.

3 Remove from the heat and stir through half the basil leaves.

4 To make the jasmine rice Put the rice, lemon grass and 4 cups of water in a pot, bring to a boil, and cook over a high heat until steam holes appear in the top of the rice. Reduce the heat to low, cover and cook over a low heat for 10 minutes, or until all the liquid is absorbed and the rice is tender. Transfer rice to bowls, spoon over curry, and scatter with remaining basil leaves.

Serves 4
Preparation 15 mins
Cooking 40 mins
Calories 597
Fat 14g

Chicken Rogan Josh

Note: With its combination of Indian spices and creamy yogurt, rogan josh is a real winner. Serve it with rice, a cooling mint raita, and some mango chutney.

Serves 4
Preparation 15 mins
Cooking 40 mins
Calories 236
Fat 9g

8 skinless boneless chicken thighs
1 tbsp vegetable oil
1 small red and 1 small green bell pepper, deseeded and thinly sliced
1 onion, thinly sliced
2 inch piece of fresh root ginger, finely chopped
2 cloves garlic, crushed
2 tbsp garam masala
1 tsp each paprika, turmeric and chili powder
4 cardamom pods, crushed
salt
1 cup Greek yogurt
2 cups canned chopped tomatoes
fresh cilantro to garnish

1 Cut each chicken thigh into 4 pieces. Heat the oil in a large heavy-based frying pan and add the peppers, onion, ginger, garlic, spices, and a good pinch of salt. Fry over a low heat for 5 minutes, or until the peppers and onion have softened.

2 Add the chicken and 2 tablespoons of the yogurt. Increase the heat to medium and cook for 4 minutes or until the yogurt is absorbed. Repeat with the rest of the yogurt.

3 Increase the heat to high, stir in the tomatoes and 1 cup of water and bring to a boil. Reduce the heat, cover, and simmer for 30 minutes or until the chicken is tender, stirring occasionally and adding more water if the sauce becomes too dry.

4 Uncover the pan, increase the heat to high and cook, stirring constantly, for 5 minutes or until the sauce thickens. Garnish with cilantro.

Drumsticks in Dill Sauce

Serves 6
Preparation 5 mins
Cooking 1 hr approx
Calories 338
Fat 7$\frac{1}{2}$g

2 tbsp butter
2 lb chicken drumsticks
1 cup chopped spring onions
3 tbsp finely chopped dill
$\frac{1}{4}$ cup lemon juice
$\frac{1}{2}$ tsp salt
$\frac{1}{4}$ tsp white pepper
1 bunch Dutch carrots, peeled
2 cups water
1 chicken stock cube
2 tbsp cornstarch
2 tbsp water

1 Heat butter in a wide-based saucepan. Add drumsticks a few at a time and brown lightly on all sides. Remove to a plate and brown remainder.

2 Add spring onions and sauté for one minute. Stir in chopped dill. Add lemon juice, return drumsticks to saucepan, sprinkle with salt and pepper.

3 Arrange the carrots over the drumsticks. Add water and stock cube. Bring to a simmer, turn down heat, cover and simmer for 40 minutes until tender.

4 Remove drumsticks and carrots with a slotted spoon and arrange on a heated platter. Blend the cornstarch with water, stir into the juices remaining in the pan. Stir over heat until sauce boils and thickens. Pour over drumsticks and carrots. Serve immediately with crusty bread.

Rabbit, Olive, and Onion Casserole

1 In a large bowl, combine rabbit, wine, oregano and bay leaves. Cover, and refrigerate overnight.
2 Drain the rabbit and reserve the marinade. Preheat oven.
3 Heat the oil in a large frypan, and brown the rabbit a few pieces at a time on both sides. Remove the rabbit and place in a casserole dish.
4 Brown the onions and garlic in the pan. Once golden, add the paprika. Stir continuously for two minutes, then add the stock and reserved marinade. Bring to the boil.
5 Pour onion and stock mixture over rabbit, add olives, and season with salt and pepper.
6 Cover and bake for one hour and 15 minutes (or until rabbit is cooked and tender). Garnish with fresh oregano, and serve with plenty of bread, to mop up juices.

1½ lb rabbit portions
2 cups dry white wine
3 sprigs fresh oregano
3 bay leaves
5 tbsp olive oil
1 cup baby onions, peeled and halved
6 cloves garlic, unpeeled
1 tbsp paprika
⅔ cup chicken stock
½ cup black olives
salt and freshly ground black pepper
fresh oregano sprigs, to garnish
crusty bread

OVEN TEMPERATURE
350°F, 180°C, GAS 4

Serves 4
Preparation 5 mins
plus marinating time
Cooking 1 hrs 30 mins
Calories 458
Fat 5½g

Cashew Nut Butter Chicken

OVEN TEMPERATURE
350°F, 180°C, GAS 4

Serves 6
Preparation 10 mins
Cooking 1 hr
Calories 451
Fat 18g

4 tbsp ghee or butter
2 cloves garlic, crushed
2 onions, minced
1 tbsp curry paste
1 tbsp ground cilantro
1/2 tsp ground nutmeg
1 1/2 lb boneless chicken thigh or
breast fillets, cut into 3/4 in cubes
1/4 cup cashews, roasted and
ground
1 1/4 cups cream (double)
2 tbsp coconut milk

1 Melt ghee or butter in a saucepan over a medium heat, add garlic and onions, and cook, stirring, for 3 minutes or until onions are golden.

2 Stir in curry paste, cilantro, and nutmeg and cook for 2 minutes or until fragrant. Add chicken and cook, stirring, for 5 minutes or until chicken is brown.

3 Add cashews, cream, and coconut milk, bring to simmering and simmer, stirring occasionally, for 40 minutes or until chicken is tender.

4 To roast cashews, spread nuts over a baking tray and bake for 5-10 minutes, or until lightly and evenly browned. Toss back and forth occasionally with a spoon to ensure even browning. Alternatively, place nuts under a medium grill and cook, tossing back and forth until roasted.

Carbonada Griolla

2 tbsp oil
1 clove garlic, crushed
1 large onion, chopped
2 lb boned shoulder of veal, cut
into ³/₄ in cubes
1 cup canned peeled tomatoes
1¹/₂ cups beef stock
1 tsp chopped thyme
2 tbsp chopped parsley
salt and pepper
1 medium potato, cubed
1 sweet potato, cubed
1¹/₂ cups cubed pumpkin
2 fresh corn cobs, cut into thick
slices
¹/₂ cup short grain rice
4 dried peaches, cut in half
4 dried pears, cut in half

1 Heat oil in a large saucepan and sauté the garlic and onion. Add veal cubes and quickly stir over high heat to brown lightly.

2 Add tomatoes, stock, thyme, parsley, and season with salt and pepper. Bring to the boil, then turn down heat and simmer for 25 minutes.

3 Add the cubed vegetables, corn, rice, and dried fruits. Cover and simmer for 25 minutes. Stir occasionally during cooking and add extra stock if necessary. Adjust seasoning before serving.

Serves 6
Preparation 12 mins
Cooking 1 hr
Calories 441
Fat 2g

Chicken Gumbo

Serves 4
Preparation 6 mins
Cooking 1 hr
Calories 328
Fat 9g

6 tbsp butter or lard and chicken fat
6-8 chicken thighs, legs or wings
1 lb okra
1 large onion, finely chopped
1 clove garlic, crushed
8 oz ham, cut in one thick slice, then in cubes
1 red bell pepper, seeded and cubed
1¹/₂ cups peeled and chopped tomatoes
1 tbsp tomato paste
¹/₂ cup dry white wine or chicken stock and water
1 bay leaf
salt and freshly ground pepper
cayenne pepper or Tabasco sauce
2 tbsp chopped parsley

1 Melt the butter or lard and chicken fat in a deep frying pan, add the chicken, and brown on all sides. Remove and keep warm. Add okra, onion, garlic, ham, and bell pepper to pan, and stir-fry until onion is soft.

2 Next, add the tomatoes, tomato paste, wine or stock, bay leaf, salt, pepper, and cayenne or Tabasco to taste.

3 Add chicken to pan, cover and simmer for 40 minutes, until chicken is tender. Scatter with parsley and serve with boiled rice.

Apple Pork Casserole

2 tbsp butter
2 onions, chopped
1 lb lean diced pork
3 large apples, peeled,
cored, and chopped
1 tbsp dried mixed herbs
3 cups chicken stock
freshly ground black pepper

Apple Sauce
1 tbsp butter
2 apples, peeled, cored, and
chopped
2 tbsp snipped fresh chives
2 cups canned tomatoes,
undrained and mashed
1 tsp cracked black peppercorns

1 Heat butter in a large frying pan and cook onions and pork over a medium heat for 5 minutes. Add apples, herbs, stock and black pepper to taste, bring to a boil, then reduce heat and simmer for 1 hour or until pork is tender. Using a slotted spoon remove pork and set aside.
2 Push liquid and solids through a sieve and return to pan with pork.
3 To make sauce, melt butter in a frying pan and cook apple over a medium heat for 2 minutes. Stir in chives and tomatoes and bring to the boil. Reduce heat and simmer for 5 minutes. Pour into pan with pork and cook over a medium heat for 5 minutes longer. Just prior to serving, sprinkle with cracked black peppercorns.

Serves 4
Preparation 10 mins
Cooking 1 hr 25 mins
Calories 422
Fat 10g

Lovely Legs and Vegetable Casserole

Oven temperature
350°F, 180°C, Gas 4

Serves 4-6
Preparation 5 mins
Cooking 1 hr
Calories 512
Fat 2¹⁄₂g

12¹⁄₂ oz jar Paul Newman's Own©
Tomato and Pesto Sauce
¹⁄₂ **cup water**
2 lb chicken drumsticks
**4 medium potatoes, peeled
and quartered**
2 tbsp olive oil
**2 tbsp finely
chopped parsley**
1¹⁄₂ **cups packet frozen peas**
1¹⁄₂ **cups canned baby corn**

1 Pour the Paul Newman's Own© Tomato and Pesto Sauce into a casserole or baking dish and stir in the water. Place lovely legs in one layer and arrange potato quarters in between. Drizzle over the olive oil and sprinkle with parsley. Cover dish with lid or foil.

2 Place in a preheated oven. Cook for 30 minutes. Lift from oven and turn the legs and potatoes. Add the peas and baby corn. Return to oven and cook uncovered for 25 minutes more or until legs and potatoes are tender when tested.

3 Serve hot with crusty bread.

Coq au Vin

1 Toss chicken in flour to coat. Shake off excess flour and set aside.

2 Heat oil in a large, nonstick frying pan over a medium heat and cook chicken in batches, turning frequently, for 10 minutes or until brown on all sides. Remove chicken from pan and drain on absorbent kitchen paper.

3 Add garlic, onions or shallots, and bacon to pan and cook, stirring, for 5 minutes or until onions are golden. Return chicken to pan, stir in stock and wine, and bring to a boil. Reduce heat, cover and simmer, stirring occasionally, for 1¼ hours or until chicken is tender. Add mushrooms and black pepper to taste and cook for 10 minutes longer.

4 lb chicken pieces
½ cup seasoned flour
2 tbsp olive oil
2 cloves garlic, crushed
12 pickling onions or shallots, peeled
8 rashers bacon, chopped
1 cup chicken stock
3 cups red wine
1½ cups button mushrooms
freshly ground black pepper

Serves 6
Preparation 5 mins
Cooking 1 hr 50 mins
Calories 677
Fat 11g

Pork Braised in Milk

Serves 4
Preparation 5 mins
Cooking 2 hrs 10 mins
Calories 406
Fat 8g

2 tbsp butter
1 tbsp vegetable oil
2 lb boneless loin pork,
rolled and tied
2 cups milk
freshly ground black pepper
3 tbsp warm water

1 Heat butter and oil in a large saucepan. When butter is foaming, add pork and brown on all sides.
2 Add milk, pepper to taste, and bring to a boil. Reduce heat to low, cover and cook for 1¹/₂-2 hours or until pork is cooked. Brush pork occasionally with milk during cooking.

3 At end of cooking time, milk should have coagulated and browned in bottom of pan. If this has not occurred, remove lid, and bring liquid to a boil. Boil until brown.
4 Remove meat from pan and set aside to cool slightly. Remove string from pork, cut into slices and arrange on a serving platter. Set aside to keep warm.
5 Remove any fat from pan, stir in water, and bring to a boil, scraping residue from base of the pan. Strain and spoon pan juices over pork to serve.

Braised Rabbit with Dried Fruits

1 Wash rabbit and pat dry. Cut into serving pieces. Season with salt and pepper. Heat oil or butter in a large, lidded frying pan or saucepan. Add rabbit pieces and quickly brown all sides on high heat.

2 Remove to a plate. Reduce heat, add onions, and cook until golden. Add water and stir to lift pan juices. Return rabbit to the pan, sprinkle in the chopped thyme and add bay leaves. Cover and simmer for 40 minutes.

3 Add the dried fruit and wine, cover, and continue to simmer for 30 minutes more, or until rabbit is tender. Add more liquid to saucepan during cooking if necessary. Taste and adjust seasoning. Uncover and stir in the cream. Simmer with lid off for 5 minutes. Serve with rice or mashed potato.

3 lb rabbit
salt and pepper
2 tbsp oil or clarified butter
6 small onions, halved
2 cups water
1 tbsp chopped, fresh thyme
2 bay leaves
1½ cups dried mixed fruit
1¼ cups red wine
½ cup cream

Serves 6
Preparation 5 mins
Cooking 1 hr 20 mins
Calories 513
Fat 7½g

Seafood and Vegetable Casseroles

Dig deep into the ocean or the earth for inspiration as you create clever casseroles using the fresh tastes of seafood and vegetables. Make a Mediterranean-style fish stew, or a lobster casserole bubbling with cheese as you feast on a fisherman's catch, or bake up a Moroccan-style potato and lemon casserole, or a vegetable stew bursting with beans as you relish these gifts from the garden. Bring the world to your front door as you try your hand at each of our seafood and vegetable casseroles. They are sure to be exciting additions to your cooking repertoire.

Moroccan Potato and Lemon Casserole

OVEN TEMPERATURE
400°F, 200°C, GAS 6

Note: A couple of
chilies and a few
spices give this
casserole of lemony
potatoes its authentic
Moroccan flavor.
Serve it with a plain
vegetable, such as
green cabbage.

Serves 4
Preparation 20 mins
Cooking 45 mins
Calories 368
Fat 16g

3 tbsp olive oil
2 onions, sliced
3 cloves garlic, chopped
2 red chilies, finely chopped
1 tsp ground cumin
1 tsp ground cilantro
2 lb waxy potatoes, such as
Charlotte,
cut into ¹/₄ inch thick slices
grated rind of 1 lemon, and
juice of 1 or 2 lemons
4 cups vegetable stock
salt and black pepper
4 tbsp sour cream to serve
3 tbsp chopped fresh parsley to
garnish

1 Preheat the oven. Heat the oil in
a flameproof and ovenproof
casserole dish. Add the onions,
garlic, chilies, cumin, and cilantro,
then gently fry for 1-2 minutes to
release their flavors.

2 Stir in the potatoes, lemon rind
and juice to taste, then add the stock
and seasoning. Bring to the boil,
cover, then cook in the oven for
40 minutes or until the vegetables
are tender and the liquid has
reduced slightly.

3 Transfer to plates and top each
serving with a spoonful of sour
cream. Sprinkle over fresh parsley
to garnish.

Rich Bean and Vegetable Stew

$^1/_2$ cup dried porcini mushrooms
3 tbsp olive oil
1$^1/_2$ cups large open
mushrooms, chopped
2 carrots, finely diced
1 large potato, diced
1 cup fine green beans, chopped
$^1/_2$ tbsp dried thyme
$^1/_2$ tbsp dried sage
2 cloves garlic, crushed
1$^1/_2$ cups red wine
2 cups vegetable stock
salt and black pepper
1 cup frozen broad beans
1 cup canned cannellini beans
1 cup canned flageolet beans

1 Cover the porcini with 2$^1/_2$ cups of boiling water, then soak for 20 minutes. Meanwhile, heat the oil in a large saucepan, then add the fresh mushrooms, carrots, potato, and green beans, and fry gently for 3-4 minutes, until slightly softened.
2 Add the thyme, sage, and garlic, the porcini with their soaking liquid, the red wine, stock, and seasoning. Bring to the boil, then simmer, uncovered, for 20 minutes or until the vegetables are tender.
3 Stir in the broad beans and simmer for a further 10 minutes or until tender. Drain and rinse the cannellini and flageolet beans, add to the mixture, then simmer for 2-3 minutes to heat through.

Note: This satisfying winter dish is perfect eaten with a hunk of crusty bread to mop up the rich red wine sauce. Serve it with a bottle of Cabernet Sauvignon.

Serves 4
Preparation 20 mins
plus 20 mins soaking
Cooking 1 hr
Calories 456
Fat 14g

Baby Vegetable Curry with Pears

Serves 6
Preparation 20 mins
Cooking 50 mins
Calories 147
Fat 9g

3 tbsp groundnut oil
2 onions, finely chopped
6 cloves garlic, finely chopped
2 pears, peeled, cored and finely chopped
3 tbsp tomato purée
2 tbsp mild curry powder
2 cups vegetable stock
salt and black pepper
1 1/2 cups baby carrots
1 1/2 cups broccoli florets
1 1/2 cups baby cauliflower, quartered
3 tbsp chopped fresh cilantro

1 Heat the oil in a large, heavy-based saucepan. Add the onions and garlic, and fry for 6-8 minutes until golden. Add the pears and fry for a further 6-8 minutes, until the pears soften and start to brown, stirring and scraping the bottom of the pan occasionally. Add a little water if the mixture becomes too dry.

2 Stir in the tomato purée and curry powder and fry for 1-2 minutes to release the flavors. Add the stock, season and bring to a boil. Reduce the heat and simmer, uncovered, for 15 minutes or until the liquid has slightly reduced.

3 Add the carrots, cover, then simmer for 5 minutes. Add the broccoli and cauliflower, cover the pan, then simmer for a further 10-15 minutes, until the vegetables are tender. Sprinkle with the cilantro just before serving.

Mediterranean Fish Stew with Rouille

**2¹/₂ lb mixed fish and shellfish,
such as cod, red mullet or
mackerel fillet, raw shell-on large
shrimp and prepared squid
1 lb Irish cooked mussels in
garlic butter sauce
2 tbsp olive oil
1 onion, finely chopped
1 tsp fennel seeds
1 cup dry white wine
2 cups canned chopped tomatoes**

Rouille
**2 cloves garlic, chopped
1 small red chili, deseeded
and chopped
3 tbsp chopped fresh cilantro
salt and black pepper
3 tbsp mayonnaise
1 tbsp olive oil**

1 First make the rouille. Crush
together the garlic, chili, and
cilantro with a pinch of salt in a
pestle and mortar. Stir in the
mayonnaise and oil, mix well, and
season to taste. Refrigerate until
needed.
2 Skin the fish, if necessary, and
cut into 2 inch chunks. Shell the
shrimp, then slit open the back of
each one and scrape out any black
vein. Rinse well. Cut the squid into
2 inch rings. Shell the mussels,
reserving a few with shells on to
garnish.

3 Heat the oil in a large heavy-
based saucepan and fry the onion
for 4 minutes to soften. Add the
fennel seeds and fry for another
minute, then add the wine,
tomatoes, and seasoning. Bring to a
boil, then simmer, uncovered, for 5
minutes, until slightly thickened.
Add the fish, squid, and shrimp and
simmer, covered, for a further 5-6
minutes, stirring occasionally, until
the shrimp are pink and everything
is cooked. Add all the mussels and
heat through. Season and serve with
the rouille.

*Note: This recipe
from the south of
France is one of the
best examples of a
rich Mediterranean
fish stew. You can
stir in as much
of the spicy, garlicky
mayonnaise as
you want.*

Serves 4
Preparation 20 mins
Cooking 20 mins
Calories 563
Fat 32g

Ratatouille in Fresh Tomato Sauce

Note: Fennel gives this quick vegetable dish a delicate aniseed flavor, while the sugar adds to the natural sweetness of the vegetables. Serve the ratatouille with long-grain rice.

Serves 4
Preparation 20 mins
Cooking 20 mins
Calories 194
Fat 12g

3 tbsp olive oil
2 cloves garlic, sliced
¹/₄ tsp chili flakes (optional)
2 red onions, sliced
1 large eggplant, cut into ¹/₂ inch cubes
2 zucchini, cut into ¹/₂ inch cubes
1 fennel bulb, cut into ¹/₂ inch cubes
1 yellow bell pepper, deseeded and cut into ¹/₂ inch cubes
6 plum tomatoes, chopped
juice of ¹/₂ lemon
1 tbsp soft light or dark brown sugar
1 tsp dried oregano
black pepper

1 Heat the oil in a large heavy-based saucepan, then add the garlic, chili flakes, if using, onions, eggplant, zucchini, and fennel. Stir well, and cook, covered, for 10 minutes, stirring often, or until the vegetables have softened.

2 Add the yellow bell pepper, tomatoes, lemon juice, sugar, oregano and seasoning to the onion mixture. Simmer, uncovered, for 10 minutes or until all the vegetables are tender, stirring occasionally.

Rich Fish Stew on Rosemary Mash

1 Rosemary mash: Remove the leaves from the rosemary sprig. Place rosemary leaves and oil in a small saucepan over a low heat. Heat until warm. Remove pan from heat. Set aside to allow the flavors to develop–if possible do this several hours in advance, the longer the leaves can steep in the oil the more pronounced the flavor. Boil or microwave potatoes until tender. Drain well. Add milk and rosemary oil. Mash. Season with white pepper and lemon juice to taste. Keep warm or reheat just prior to serving.

2 Heat oil in a large deep-sided nonstick frying pan over a medium heat. Add leek and garlic. Cook, stirring, for 1-2 minutes or until soft. Add oregano, mushrooms and celery. Cook, stirring, for 2-3 minutes. Stir in tomato paste. Cook for 3-4 minutes or until it becomes deep red and develops a rich aroma.

3 Stir in zucchini, tomatoes, and wine. Bring to a boil. Reduce heat. Simmer, stirring occasionally, for 5 minutes or until mixture starts to thicken.

4 Add fish. Cook for 6 minutes or until fish is just cooked–take care not to overcook or the fish will fall apart. Stir in basil and parsley.

5 To serve, place a mound of mash on each serving plate. Top with fish stew. Accompany with a green salad or steamed green vegetables of your choice.

2 tsp olive oil
1 leek, chopped
1 clove garlic, crushed
1 tsp ground oregano
4 flat mushrooms, sliced
1 stalk celery, sliced
1 tbsp no-added-salt tomato paste
2 zucchini, sliced
2 cups canned no-added-salt diced tomatoes
$^1/_2$ cup white wine
1 lb firm white fish fillets (gemfish, ling, barramundi, sea bass, or blue-eye cod)
1 tbsp chopped fresh basil
1 tbsp chopped fresh parsley

Rosemary Mash
1 sprig fresh rosemary
2 tsp olive oil
2 large potatoes, chopped
$^1/_4$ cup low-fat milk, warmed ground white pepper lemon juice, optional

Serves 4
Preparation 8 mins
Cooking 25 mins plus 15 mins for Mash and potato preparation
Calories 304
Fat 8g

Braised Vegetables with a Cheddar Crust

OVEN TEMPERATURE
400°F, 200°C, GAS 6

Note: A vegetarian main course with a rich deep flavor that will satisfy even the most determined carnivores.

Serves 6
Preparation 30 mins
Cooking 1 hr 35 mins
Calories 522
Fat 34g

4 tbsp olive oil
2 tbsp butter
2 red onions, thinly sliced
1 head celery, thickly sliced
2 large carrots, thickly sliced
2 cloves garlic, crushed
salt and black pepper
4 large open mushrooms, sliced
3 red bell peppers, deseeded
and cut into strips
1 tsp each dried oregano
and thyme
2 eggplant, thickly sliced
1 cup vegetable stock

Crust
2 cups plain flour
2 tsp baking powder
5 tbsp chilled butter, cubed
5 tbsp grated Cheddar
2 tbsp fresh breadcrumbs
$1/2$ cup double cream
2 tbsp chopped fresh parsley
1 tsp dried oregano

1 Heat 1 tablespoon of the oil with half the butter in a large frying pan. Add the onions, celery, carrots, and garlic. Cook for 10 minutes, stirring often. Season, remove from the pan and set aside.
2 Preheat the oven. Heat another tablespoon of oil in the pan, add the mushrooms, bell peppers, oregano, and thyme and cook for 5 minutes, stirring often. Season and add to the other vegetables. Heat the remaining oil and fry the eggplant for 3 minutes, turning once, to brown.
3 Grease a lasagna dish with the rest of the butter. Add the vegetables, pour in the stock and loosely cover with foil. Cook for 40 minutes. Remove the foil, stir, and cook for a further 5 minutes or until tender.
4 Meanwhile, make the crust. Sift the flour and baking powder into a bowl. Rub in the butter, until the texture resembles coarse breadcrumbs. Mix in the Cheddar, breadcrumbs, cream, parsley, and oregano, and season. Increase the oven temperature to 450°F/230°C/Gas Mark 8. Spoon the crust mixture over the vegetables. Cook for 20 minutes or until golden. Set aside to rest for 10 minutes before serving.

Lobster Cheese Casserole

1 lb lobster meat, diced
2 tbsp butter
$^1/_4$ cup flour
$^3/_4$ cup milk
1$^1/_4$ cups whipping cream
$^1/_2$ cup grated Cheddar cheese
$^1/_2$ tsp salt
$^3/_4$ cup green bell pepper, diced
$^1/_4$ cup grated Cheddar cheese, extra
pinch paprika

1 Place lobster in a greased 4 cup casserole. Over low heat, melt butter, lend in flour and slowly add milk and cream. Cook, stirring constantly until mixture is thick and smooth. Add the cheese, salt, and green bell pepper. Stir until cheese melts. Pour over lobster. Sprinkle extra cheese over top and garnish with paprika. Bake in hot oven for 15 minutes. Broil for 2 minutes to brown the top.

OVEN TEMPERATURE
350°F, 180°C, GAS 4

Serves 4-6
Preparation 10 mins
Cooking 28 mins
Calories 323
Fat 12$^1/_2$g

Seafood Casserole

1 tbsp olive oil
1 medium onion,
roughly chopped
1 leek, finely chopped
2 cloves garlic, crushed
2 cups canned tomatoes
2 bay leaves
1 tbsp parsley, chopped
$1/4$ cup dry white wine
salt and freshly ground
black pepper
2 lb assorted fish and seafood*
2 tbsp oregano, chopped

*Note: Suitable fish
and seafood include
red mullet, monk
fish, sea bream, cod,
calamari,
mussels, shelled
shrimp, and clams.*

Serves 4-6
Preparation 6 mins
Cooking 40 mins
Calories 228
Fat 1g

1 Heat the oil in a flame-proof
casserole dish. Sauté the onion, leek,
and garlic until softened and slightly
golden.
2 Add the tomatoes, bay leaves,
parsley, wine, salt, and freshly
ground black pepper. Bring to a boil,
cover, and simmer gently for 20
minutes.
3 Stir in any firm-fleshed fish and
simmer for five minutes. Stir in the
remaining soft-fleshed fish, placing
shell fish on the top.
4 Cover with a lid and continue
cooking for 5-7 minutes (until the
fish is tender) and the shell fish have
opened (discarding any that remain
closed).
5 Serve garnished with fresh oregano.

Glossary

acidulated water: water with added acid, such as lemon juice or vinegar, which prevents discoloration of ingredients, particularly fruit or vegetables. The proportion of acid to water is 1 teaspoon per 300mL.

al dente: Italian cooking term for ingredients that are cooked until tender but still firm to the bite; usually applied to pasta.

americaine: method of serving seafood–usually lobster and monkfish–in a sauce flavored with olive oil, aromatic herbs, tomatoes, white wine, fish stock, brandy, and tarragon.

anglaise: cooking style for simple cooked dishes such as boiled vegetables. Assiette anglaise is a plate of cold cooked meats.

antipasto: Italian for "before the meal," it denotes an assortment of cold meats, vegetables, and cheeses, often marinated, served as an hors d'oeuvre. A typical antipasto might include salami, prosciutto, marinated artichoke hearts, anchovy fillets, olives, tuna fish, and Provolone cheese.

au gratin: food sprinkled with breadcrumbs, often covered with cheese sauce, and browned until a crisp coating forms.

balsamic vinegar: a mild, extremely fragrant, wine-based vinegar made in northern Italy. Traditionally, the vinegar is aged for at least seven years in a series of casks made of various woods.

baste: to moisten food while it is cooking by spooning or brushing on liquid or fat.

baine marie: a saucepan standing in a large pan, which is filled with boiling water to keep liquids at simmering point. A double boiler will do the same job.

beat: to stir thoroughly and vigorously.

beurre manie: equal quantities of butter and flour kneaded together and added a little at a time to thicken a stew or casserole.

bird: see paupiette.

blanc: a cooking liquid made by adding flour and lemon juice to water in order to keep certain vegetables from discoloring as they cook.

blanch: to plunge into boiling water and then, in some cases, into cold water. Fruits and nuts are blanched to remove skin easily.

blanquette: a white stew of lamb, veal, or chicken, bound with egg yolks and cream and accompanied by onion and mushrooms.

blend: to mix thoroughly.

bonne femme: dishes cooked in the traditional French "housewife" style. Chicken and pork bonne femme are garnished with bacon, potatoes, and baby onion; fish bonne femme with mushrooms in a white wine sauce.

bouquet garni: a bunch of herbs, usually consisting of sprigs of parsley, thyme, marjoram, rosemary, a bay leaf, peppercorns, and cloves, tied in muslin and used to flavor stews and casseroles.

braise: to cook whole or large pieces of poultry, game, fish, meat, or vegetables in a small amount of wine, stock, or other liquid in a closed pot. Often the main ingredient is first browned in fat and then cooked in a low oven or very slowly on top of the stove. Braising suits tough meats and older birds and produces a mellow, rich sauce.

broil: the American term for grilling food.

brown: cook in a small amount of fat until brown.

burghul (also bulgur): a type of cracked wheat, where the kernels are steamed and dried before being crushed.

buttered: to spread with softened or melted butter.

butterfly: to slit a piece of food in half horizontally, cutting it almost through so that when opened it resembles butterfly wings. Chops, large shrimp (prawns), and thick fish fillets are often butterflied so that they cook more quickly.

buttermilk: a tangy, low-fat cultured milk product whose slight acidity makes it an ideal marinade base for poultry.

calzone: a semicircular pocket of pizza dough, stuffed with meat or vegetables, sealed and baked.

caramelize: to melt sugar until it is a golden brown syrup.

champignons: small mushrooms, usually canned.

chasseur: (hunter) a French cooking style in which meat and chicken dishes are cooked with mushrooms, shallots, white wine, and often tomato.

clarify: to melt butter and drain the oil off the sediment.

coat: to cover with a thin layer of flour, sugar, nuts, crumbs, poppy or sesame seeds, cinnamon sugar, or a few of the ground spices.

concasser: to chop coarsely, usually tomatoes.

confit: from the French verb confire, meaning to preserve. Food that is made into a preserve by cooking very slowly and thoroughly until tender. In the case of meat, such as duck or goose, it is cooked in its own fat, and covered with it so that it does not come into contact with the air. Vegetables such as onions are good in confit.

consomme: a clear soup usually made from beef.

coulis: a thin puree, usually of fresh or cooked fruit or vegetables, which is soft enough to pour (couler means "to run"). A coulis may be rough-textured or very smooth.

court bouillon: the liquid in which fish, poultry, or meat is cooked. It usually consists of water with bay leaf, onion, carrots, and salt and freshly ground black pepper to taste. Other additives can include wine, vinegar, stock, garlic, or spring onions (scallions).

couscous: cereal processed from semolina into pellets, traditionally steamed and served with meat and vegetables in the classic North African stew of the same name.

cruciferous vegetables: certain members of the mustard, cabbage, and turnip families with cross-shaped flowers and strong aromas and flavors.

cream: to make soft, smooth, and creamy by rubbing with back of spoon or by beating with mixer. Usually applied to fat and sugar.

croutons: small toasted or fried cubes of bread.

crudites: raw vegetables, whether cut in slices or sticks to nibble plain or with a dipping sauce, or shredded and tossed as salad with a simple dressing.

cube: to cut into small pieces with six equal sides.

curdle: to cause milk or sauce to separate into solid and liquid. Example, overcooked egg mixtures.

daikon radish: (also called mooli) a long white Japanese radish.

Dark sesame oil: (also called Oriental sesame oil) dark polyunsaturated oil with a low burning point, used for seasoning. Do not replace with lighter sesame oil.

deglaze: to dissolve congealed cooking juices or glaze on the bottom of a pan by adding a liquid, then scraping and stirring vigorously while bringing the liquid to the boil. Juices may be used to make gravy or to add to sauce.

degrease: to skim grease from the surface of liquid. If possible the liquid should be chilled so the fat solidifies. If not, skim off most of the fat with a large metal spoon, then trail strips of paper towel on the surface of the liquid to remove any remaining globules.

devilled: a dish or sauce that is highly seasoned with a hot ingredient such as mustard, Worcestershire sauce or cayenne pepper.

dice: to cut into small cubes.

dietary fiber: a plant-cell material that is undigested or only partially digested in the human body, but which promotes healthy digestion of other food matter.

dissolve: mix a dry ingredient with liquid until absorbed.

dredge: to coat with a dry ingredient, as flour or sugar.

drizzle: to pour in a fine thread-like stream over a surface.

dust: to sprinkle or coat lightly with flour or icing sugar.

Dutch oven: a heavy casserole with a lid usually made from cast iron or pottery.

emulsion: a mixture of two liquids that are not mutually soluble– for example, oil and water.

entree: in Europe, the "entry" or hors d'oeuvre; in North America entree means the main course.

fillet: special cut of beef, lamb, pork, or veal; breast of poultry and game; fish cut of the bone lengthways.

flake: to break into small pieces with a fork.

flame: to ignite warmed alcohol over food.

fold in: a gentle, careful combining of a light or delicate mixture with a heavier mixture using a metal spoon.

fricassee: a dish in which poultry, fish, or vegetables are bound together with a white or veloute sauce. In Britain and the United States, the name applies to an old-fashioned dish of chicken in a creamy sauce.

galette: sweet or savoury mixture shaped as a flat round.

garnish: to decorate food, usually with something edible.

gastrique: caramelized sugar deglazed with vinegar and used in fruit-flavored savoury sauces, in such dishes as duck with orange.

glaze: a thin coating of beaten egg, syrup, or aspic which is brushed over pastry, fruits, or cooked meats.

gluten: a protein in flour that is developed when dough is kneaded, making it elastic.

gratin: a dish cooked in the oven or under the grill so that it develops a brown crust. Breadcrumbs or cheese may be sprinkled on top first. Shallow gratin dishes ensure a maximum area of crust.

grease: to rub or brush lightly with oil or fat.

joint: to cut poultry, game, or small animals into serving pieces by dividing at the joint.

julienne: to cut food into match-like strips.

knead: to work dough using heel of hand with a pressing motion, while stretching and folding the dough.

line: to cover the inside of a container with paper, to protect or aid in removing mixture.

infuse: to immerse herbs, spices, or other flavorings in hot liquid to flavor it. Infusion takes from two to five minutes, depending on the flavoring. The liquid should be very hot but not boiling.

jardiniere: a garnish of garden vegetables, typically carrots, pickling onions, French beans, and turnips.

lights: lungs of an animal, used in various meat preparations such as pâtes and faggots.

macerate: to soak food in liquid to soften.

marinade: a seasoned liquid, usually an oil and acid mixture, in which meats or other foods are soaked to soften and give more flavor.

marinara: Italian "sailor's style" cooking that does not apply to any particular combination of ingredients. Marinara tomato sauce for pasta is most familiar.

marinate: to let food stand in a marinade to season and tenderize.

mask: to cover cooked food with sauce.

melt: to heat until liquified.

mince: to grind into very small pieces.

mix: to combine ingredients by stirring.

monounsaturated fats: one of three types of fats found in foods. Are believed not to raise the level of cholesterol in the blood.

nicoise: a garnish of tomatoes, garlic, and black olives; a salad with anchovy, tuna and French beans is typical.

non-reactive pan: a cooking pan whose surface does not chemically react with food. Materials used include stainless steel, enamel, glass, and some alloys.

noisette: small "nut" of lamb cut from boned loin or rack that is rolled, tied, and cut in neat slices. Noisette also means flavored with hazelnuts, or butter cooked to a nut brown colour.

normande: a cooking style for fish, with a garnish of shrimp, mussels, and mushrooms in a white wine cream sauce; for poultry and meat, a sauce with cream, Calvados, and apple.

olive oil: various grades of oil extract from olives. Extra virgin olive oil has a full, fruity flavor and the lowest acidity. Virgin olive oil is slightly higher in acidity and lighter in flavor. Pure olive oil is a processed blend of olive oils and has the highest acidity and lightest taste.

panade: a mixture for binding stuffings and dumplings, notably quenelles, often of choux pastry or simply breadcrumbs. A panade may also be made of frangipane, pureed potatoes, or rice.

papillote: to cook food in oiled or buttered greasepoof paper or aluminium foil. Also a decorative frill to cover bone ends of chops and poultry drumsticks.

parboil: to boil or simmer until part cooked (i.e. cooked further than when blanching).

pare: to cut away outside covering.

pâte: a paste of meat or seafood used as a spread for toast or crackers.

paupiette: a thin slice of meat, poultry, or fish spread with a savoury stuffing and rolled. In the United States this is also called "bird" and in Britain an "olive."

peel: to strip away outside covering.

plump: to soak in liquid or moisten thoroughly until full and round.

poach: to simmer gently in enough hot liquid to cover, using care to retain shape of food.

polyunsaturated fat: one of the three types of fats found in food. These exist in large quantities in such vegetable oils as safflower, sunflower, corn, and soya bean. These fats lower the level of cholesterol in the blood.

puree: a smooth paste, usually of vegetables or fruits, made by putting foods through a sieve, food mill, or liquefying in a blender or food processor.

ragout: traditionally a well-seasoned, rich stew containing meat, vegetables, and wine. Nowadays, a term applied to any stewed mixture.

ramekins: small oval or round individual baking dishes.

reconstitute: to put moisture back into dehydrated foods by soaking in liquid.

reduce: to cook over a very high heat, uncovered, until the liquid is reduced by evaporation.

refresh: to cool hot food quickly, either under running water or

by plunging it into iced water, to stop it cooking. Particularly for vegetables, and occasionally for shellfish.

rice vinegar: mild, fragrant vinegar that is less sweet than cider vinegar and not as harsh as distilled malt vinegar. Japanese rice vinegar is milder than the Chinese variety.

roulade: a piece of meat, usually pork or veal, that is spread with stuffing, rolled, and often braised or poached. A roulade may also be a sweet or savoury mixture that is baked in a Swiss roll tin or paper case, filled with a contrasting filling, and rolled.

rubbing-in: a method of incorporating fat into flour, by use of fingertips only. Also incorporates air into mixture.

safflower oil: the vegetable oil that contains the highest proportion of polyunsaturated fats.

salsa: a juice derived from the main ingredient being cooked or a sauce added to a dish to enhance its flavor. In Italy the term is often used for pasta sauces; in Mexico the name usually applies to uncooked sauces served as an accompaniment, especially to corn chips.

saturated fats: one of the three types of fats found in foods. These exist in large quantities in animal products, coconut, and palm oils; they raise the level of cholesterol in the blood. As high cholesterol levels may cause heart disease, saturated fat consumption is recommended to be less than 15% of calories provided by the daily diet.

sauté: to cook or brown in small amount of hot fat.

score: to mark food with cuts, notches of lines to prevent curling or to make food more attractive.

scald: to bring just to boiling point, usually for milk. Also to rinse with boiling water.

sear: to brown surface quickly over high heat in hot dish.

seasoned flour: flour with salt and pepper added.

sift: to shake a dry, powdered substance through a sieve or sifter to remove any lumps and give lightness.

simmer: to cook food gently in liquid that bubbles steadily just below boiling point so that the food cooks in even heat without breaking up.

singe: to quickly flame poultry to remove all traces of feathers after plucking.

skim: to remove a surface layer (often of impurities and scum) from a liquid with a metal spoon or small ladle.

slivered: sliced in long, thin pieces, usually refers to nuts, especially almonds.

soften: ie: gelatine. Sprinkle over cold water and allow to gel (soften) then dissolve and liquefy.

souse: to cover food, particularly fish, in wine vinegar and spices and cook slowly; the food is cooled in the same liquid. Sousing gives food a pickled flavor.

steep: to soak in warm or cold liquid in order to soften food and draw out strong flavors or impurities.

stir-fry: to cook thin slices of meat and vegetable over a high heat in a small amount of oil, stirring constantly to even cooking in a short time. Traditionally cooked in a wok, however a heavy based frying pan may be used.

stock: a liquid containing flavors, extracts, and nutrients of bones, meat, fish, or vegetables.

stud: to adorn with; for example, baked ham studded with whole cloves.

sugo: an Italian sauce made from the liquid or juice extracted from fruit or meat during cooking.

sweat: to cook sliced or chopped food, usually vegetables, in a little fat and no liquid over very low heat. Foil is pressed on top so that the food steams in its own juices, usually before being added to other dishes.

timbale: a creamy mixture of vegetables or meat baked in a mould. French for "kettledrum"; also denotes a drum-shaped baking dish.

thicken: to make a thin, smooth paste by mixing together arrowroot, corn flour, or flour with an equal amount of cold water; stir into hot liquid, cook, stirring until thickened.

toss: to gently mix ingredients with two forks or fork and spoon.

total fat: the individual daily intake of all three fats previously described in this glossary. Nutritionists recommend that fats provide no more than 35% of the energy in the diet.

vine leaves: tender, lightly flavored leaves of the grapevine, used in ethnic cuisine as wrappers for savoury mixtures. As the leaves are usually packed in brine, they should be well rinsed before use.

whip: to beat rapidly, incorporate air, and produce expansion.

zest: thin outer layer of citrus fruits containing the aromatic citrus oil. It is usually thinly pared with a vegetable peeler, or grated with a zester or grater to separate it from the bitter white pith underneath.

Weights & Measures

Cooking is not an exact science: one does not require finely calibrated scales, pipettes, and scientific equipment to cook, yet the conversion to metric measures in some countries and its interpretations must have intimidated many a good cook.

Weights are given in the recipes only for ingredients such as meats, fish, poultry, and some vegetables. Though a few grams/ounces one way or another will not affect the success of your dish.

Though recipes have been tested using the Australian Standard 250mL cup, 20mL tablespoon, and 5mL teaspoon, they will work just as well with the US and Canadian 8 fl oz cup, or the UK 300mL cup. We have used graduated cup measures in preference to tablespoon measures so that proportions are always the same. Where tablespoon measures have been given, these are not crucial measures, so using the smaller tablespoon of the US or UK will not affect the recipe's success. At least we all agree on the teaspoon size.

For breads, cakes, and pastries, the only area which might cause concern is where eggs are used, as proportions will then vary. If working with a 250mL or 300mL cup, use large eggs (65g/2$^1/_4$oz), adding a little more liquid to the recipe for 300mL cup measures if it seems necessary. Use the medium-sized eggs (55g/2oz) with 8 fl oz cup measure. A graduated set of measuring cups and spoons is recommended, the cups in particular for measuring dry ingredients. Remember to level such ingredients to ensure their accuracy.

English measures

All measurements are similar to Australian with two exceptions: the English cup measures 300mL/10$^1/_2$fl oz, whereas the Australian cup measure 250mL/8$^3/_4$fl oz. The English tablespoon (the Australian dessertspoon) measures 14.8mL/$^1/_2$fl oz against the Australian tablespoon of 20mL/$^3/_4$fl oz.

American measures

The American reputed pint is 16 fl oz, a quart is equal to 32 fl oz and the American gallon, 128 fl oz. The Imperial measurement is 20 fl oz to the pint, 40 fl oz a quart and 160 fl oz one gallon. The American tablespoon is equal to 14.8 mL/$^1/_2$fl oz, the teaspoon is 5 mL/$^1/_6$fl oz. The cup measure is 250 mL/8$^3/_4$fl oz, the same as Australia.

Dry measures

All the measures are level, so when you have filled a cup or spoon, level it off with the edge of a knife. The scale below is the "cook's equivalent"; it is not an exact conversion of metric to imperial measurement. To calculate the exact metric equivalent yourself, multiply ounces by 28.349523 to obtain grams, or divide 28.349523 grams to obtain ounces.

Metric	Imperial
g = grams	oz = ounces
kg = kilograms	lb = pound
15g	$^1/_2$ oz
20g	$^2/_3$ oz
30g	1 oz
55g	2 oz
85g	3 oz
115g	4 oz/$^1/_4$ lb
125g	4$^1/_2$ oz
140/145g	5 oz
170g	6 oz
200g	7 oz
225g	8 oz/$^1/_2$ lb
315g	11 oz
340g	12 oz/$^3/_4$ lb
370g	13 oz
400g	14 oz
425g	15 oz
455g	16 oz/1 lb
1,000g/1kg	35.3 oz/2.2 lb
1.5kg	3.3 lb

Oven temperatures

The Celsius temperatures given here are not exact; they have been rounded off and are given as a guide only. Follow the manufacturer's temperature guide, relating it to oven description given in the recipe. Remember gas ovens are hottest at the top, electric ovens at the bottom, and convection-fan forced ovens are usually even throughout. We included Regulo numbers for gas cookers which may assist.

To convert °C to °F, multiply °C by 9, and divide by 5 then add 32.

Oven temperatures

	C°	F°	Gas regulo
Very slow	120	250	1
Slow	150	300	2
Moderately slow	160	325	3
Moderate	180	350	4
Moderately hot	190-200	370-400	5-6
Hot	210-220	410-440	6-7
Very hot	230	450	8
Super hot	250-290	475-500	9-10

Cake dish sizes

metric	imperial
15 cm	6 in
18 cm	7 in
20 cm	8 in
23 cm	9 in

Loaf dish sizes

metric	imperial
23x12 cm	9x5 in
25x8 cm	10x3 in
28x18 cm	11x7 in

Liquid measures

metric mL millilitres	imperial fl oz fluid ounce	cup and spoon
5mL	$^1/_6$ fl oz	1 teaspoon
20mL	$^2/_3$ fl oz	1 tablespoon
30mL	1 fl oz	1 tablespoon plus 2 teaspoons
55mL	2 fl oz	$^1/_4$ cup
85mL	3 fl oz	
115mL	4 fl oz	$^1/_2$ cup
125mL	$4^1/_2$ fl oz	
150mL	$5^1/_4$ fl oz	
170mL	6 fl oz	$^3/_4$ cup
225mL	8 fl oz	1 cup
300mL	$10^1/_2$ fl oz	
370mL	13 fl oz	
400mL	14 fl oz	$1^3/_4$ cups
455mL	16 fl oz	2 cups
570mL	20 fl oz	$2^1/_2$ cups
1 litre	35.3 fl oz	4 cups

Cup measurements

One cup is equal to the following weights.

	Metric	Imperial
Almonds, flaked	85g	3 oz
Almonds, slivered, ground	125g	$4^1/_2$ oz
Almonds, kernel	155g	$5^1/_2$ oz
Apples, dried, chopped	125g	$4^1/_2$ oz

	Metric	Imperial
Apricots, dried, chopped	190g	$6^3/_4$ oz
Breadcrumbs, packet	125g	$4^1/_2$ oz
Breadcrumbs, soft	55g	2 oz
Cheese, grated	115g	4 oz
Choc bits	$155^1/_2$g	5 oz
Coconut, desiccated	90g	3 oz
Cornflakes	30g	1 oz
Currants	$155^1/_2$g	5 oz
Flour	115g	4 oz
Fruit, dried (mixed, sultanas etc)	170g	6 oz
Ginger, crystallized, glace	250g	8 oz
Honey, treacle, golden syrup	315g	11 oz
Mixed peel	225g	8 oz
Nuts, chopped	115g	4 oz
Prunes, chopped	225g	8 oz
Rice, cooked	155g	$5^1/_2$ oz
Rice, uncooked	225g	8 oz
Rolled oats	90g	3 oz
Sesame seeds	115g	4 oz
Shortening (butter, margarine)	225g	8 oz
Sugar, brown	155g	$5^1/_2$ oz
Sugar, granulated or caster	225g	8 oz
Sugar, sifted icing	155g	$5^1/_2$ oz
Wheatgerm	60g	2 oz

Length

Some of us still have trouble converting imperial length to metric. In this scale, measures have been rounded off to the easiest-to-use and most acceptable figures. To obtain the exact metric equivalent in converting inches to centimeters, multiply inches by 2.54 whereby 1 inch equals 25.4 millimeters and 1 millimeter equals 0.03937 inches.

Metric mm=millimetres cm=centimetres	Imperial in = inches ft = feet
5 mm, 0.5 cm	$^1/_4$ in
10 mm, 1.0 cm	$^1/_2$ in
20 mm, 2.0 cm	$^3/_4$ in
2.5 cm	1 in
5 cm	2 in
$7^1/_2$ cm	3 in
10 cm	4 in
$12^1/_2$ cm	5 in
15 cm	6 in
18 cm	7 in
20 cm	8 in
23 cm	9 in
25 cm	10 in
28 cm	11 in
30 cm	12 in, 1ft

Index